I0425664

The
Expectant
Father's
Handbook

The Expectant Father's Handbook

A Simple Guide to Your New Life

Running Press

What kind of father do you want to be?

WHILE FATHERHOOD IS POSSIBLY THE MOST important role a man will play in his lifetime, many men have been culturally and emotionally separated from pregnancy and the childbearing process. A man can only imagine how it feels physically or emotionally to have a baby growing inside of him. Generally excluded by the medical profession, physically alienated from issues of reproduction, and presented as useless or delinquent by the media, men are faced with ill-defined fathering roles to follow. In order for a man to be a successful father, these barriers must come down. But how? How does he compensate for the stereotype of the bumbling, incompetent sidekick? Must he resort to walking through the nine months with a pillow stuffed under his shirt? Where can an expectant father go to learn how to get over such hurdles? Your first steps to a happy, healthy fatherhood should be taken with *The Expectant Father's Handbook.*

Don't let the popular notion of an expectant father's futility become a self-fulfilling prophecy. You have the power to make your situation different. Remember that the healthiest pregnancy is couple-focused, not simply mother-focused. While there are significant physical, emotional, and cultural obstacles to face during expectant fatherhood, they can be overcome through commitment to your partner's healthy pregnancy, understanding of what you're each experiencing, and having patience with both your partner and yourself. Start by listening to your partner, encouraging her, and helping her stay healthy, calm, and happy. Your partner is the closest link you have to your baby, and giving her the emotional and physical support she needs will ease her adjustment to the pregnancy and contribute to your baby's good health. Be prepared as an expectant father to work twice as hard to get half the support, recognition, and attention your partner will receive. Women are congratulated by complete strangers who see their rounded belly, yet no one knows a man is expecting simply by looking at him.

UE

Century la... tw...
Super Bowls will
warm, ...arant...

NEW ORLEANS — ...
ever the NFL owners g... ...n-
select a Super Bowl si... ...ey
laugh nervously abou... ...
the year of the close c... ...4,
Philadelphia, of a... ...
bid to host a goose-bum... ...
Bowl and almost got it... ...
cities competing, it too... ...
lots before Pasadena... ...
and San Diego were... ...
Super Bowls XXI a... ...
"At one point ... ...
locked between ... ...
Philadelphia, ...
the NFL's s... ...
tor. Phila... ...
balmy ...
brought ...

Pro fo...

...We'll party
...an forget th
...on's arm-twi
...ering effort that
...Bowl XXII for u
...n Diego. After Pasa
...Super Bowl XXI, San
...nd Miami were still d
...d after seven ballots.
...ting, husting votes,
...ed the owners to go
...mple majority f

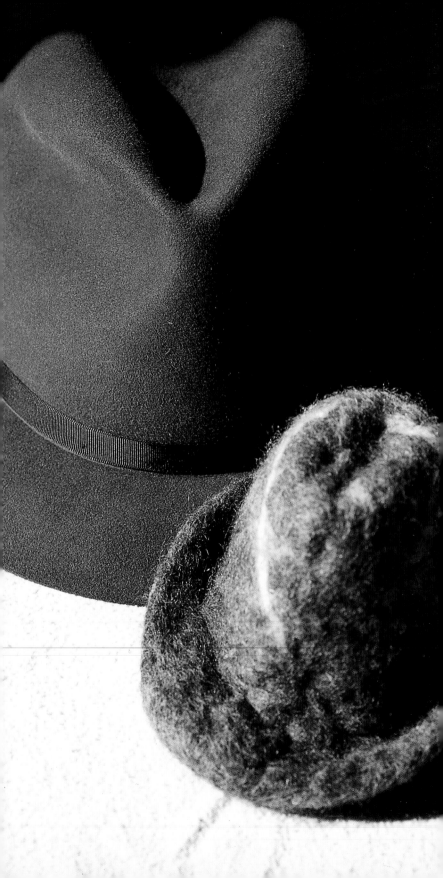

Let people know! When you make the pregnancy yours as well as your partner's, you set the standard for your involvement in the life of your child for years to come. Fatherhood begins well before your child is actually born.

Educating yourself, communicating honestly with your partner, and recognizing that the changes you'll go through will be just as varied as your partner's are steps that will bring you closer to your own "pregnancy" and to your baby. Following are the ABCs of expectant fatherhood: issues, emotions, and concerns you may encounter during the pregnancy and ways to constructively confront them. They've been compiled with the help of many fathers to reassure and support you—voices of experience with a sense of humor.

Share in the experience. Because you're expecting, too!

"I just know I can
be a great dad.
I am determined to
be a terrific father,
a fun dad."

Don't be surprised by the **anxiety** you feel during pregnancy. There is a lot to worry about: your baby's and your partner's health, decisions like what kind of stroller to buy, and concerns such as whether or not you'll ever see a movie in a theater again! There will be huge **adjustments** to make in your new life—and this is understandably scary—so don't keep your fears to yourself. Nothing will be resolved by your silence, and your fears may explode in **argument**. Just as you cannot expect to understand exactly what she is experiencing, you must not **assume** that your partner understands all the issues you're dealing with. Talk to her about them openly and make her **aware**. She's probably been having similar thoughts. If you can't **address** the issues immediately with your partner, first seek the **advice** of your male friends who've been through their own pregnancy. They will **appreciate** being involved in such a significant event in your life, and the camaraderie will ease your mind.

It may seem as if there is always something you need to **buy** for the **baby**. From rattles and **booties** to strollers and cribs, having a baby is not cheap. While there is no way to avoid the accumulation of **bills**, there are ways to ease the expenses. First, maintain a **balanced** perspective, and try not to get overwhelmed. Second, recognize that there is nothing wrong with asking for help. Friends or family members with children will probably be happy to loan or even give you some **basics** their children have outgrown. Frequent second-hand stores and watch the newspapers for inexpensive used furniture items, car seats, walking or jogging strollers, etc., but check that these items meet current safety standards. **Baby showers** also provide you with much-needed items. If you like to **build** things, this is the perfect time to hit the garage. A crib, chair, or changing table you've made yourself is not only practical but a beautiful gift your child will cherish throughout his or her life.

"For the first month or so after Patti broke the news I was this close to panic. But nine months gives everyone plenty of time to get into it."

There are things that you will not be able to **control** during the pregnancy, namely the **changes** and **challenges** that you and especially your partner will be presented with. While you both may experience similar emotions, frustrations, and fears as individuals, you will probably handle them differently. This, compounded by the physical changes she is experiencing that are so alien to you, may lead to **conflict**, and you may feel that the pregnancy is completely out of your hands. Remain **calm**, and open the lines of **communication** with your partner. Remember that your role as expectant father is a **complex** one, and that the best way for you to feel **comfortable** is to inform yourself and to **contribute** to the pregnancy in the ways that you can instead of focusing on the ways that you cannot. Build things for your new baby, record music, write letters to your growing child. **Contact** with other expectant fathers and with fathers with babies may offer you solace and support.

Your partner needs to know that you are **dedicated** to the pregnancy. **Denial** of the pregnancy, your partner's needs, or your own is not effective. There may be points at which your partner has **doubts** about herself, you, or the baby. Showing her you are committed to her, the pregnancy, and the baby will help her to regain confidence. Planning for the baby's arrival is a good way to become involved in the pregnancy and to avoid last minute **decisions** and **disagreements**. For example, decide whether you prefer cloth or disposable **diapers**. Choose a wallpaper for the baby's room. Clean the house or yard. If you've been talking about painting the kitchen, do it now. Pay attention to your partner's **diet**. Helping her eat right is a great way to contribute to her and the baby's good health. Demonstrate your love by taking her on a **date**—perhaps a quick day trip to a romantic spot. Remember, you are the one person who can most thoroughly put your partner at ease, the one person she **depends** upon the most. Commit yourself to being involved all the way through to **delivery**.

"I'd never tell this to my dad but many of the best lessons he taught me were by bad example . . .

". . . For one thing, I plan
to be around more
than he was.
Just having your dad
there is important."

Don't let the people around you **exclude** you from your own pregnancy. Let everyone know from the beginning that you are **essential** and will be involved in the pregnancy and birth process at **every** step of the way. Set the standard **early** so that friends, relatives, and medical personnel understand your **equal** partnership in the pregnancy. Remember that your role as expectant father, like that of an expectant mother, is an **evolving** one. Parenthood is a gradual process, beginning with conception, that involves an **endless** series of decisions and adjustments. The decisions you make now help shape your family's future. This is no small responsibility! Take the time to think about how you want your family to be: imagine the future and the **environment** you want to create for your child. Work toward this future, but don't rush the process or have unreasonable **expectations**. Allow yourself to **enjoy** and be thoroughly **engrossed** in the daily processes, recognizing that it takes time to become a parent. These small **experiences** will **enrich** you and lead you in the right direction.

As you and your partner progress through the pregnancy, you will define more clearly your roles within the **family**. These definitions will change and grow after your child is born, so don't pressure yourself to have the perfect family **firmly** established by the end of nine months. It will take years. For better or for worse, **friends** and family will come out of the woodwork and subject you to advice, suggestions, and criticism, whether you've asked for it or not. Don't be **frustrated** by unsolicited advice; **focus** on the important and **forget** the irrelevant. Be kind but **firm**, letting them know that you appreciate their experiences, but that you will **forge** your own path to **fatherhood**.

You may find, once the baby is born, that you grow apart from friends who don't have children. Spend time and have **fun** with these and all of your friends during your pregnancy. Let them know you will be busy once the baby arrives, but that you want them to continue to be involved in your lives.

20

"I knew I would get cranky and jealous if I had to stay home with Charlie while Chaz went to the gym, so we rearranged the dining room into an exercise area. Now we can both do our routines with Charlie right there in the room with us."

Many men admit they feel responsible for the pain or discomfort their partners feel during pregnancy, as if they had done something injurious to their mate. There is nothing to feel **guilty** about. Your pregnancy is a joint decision and responsibility. You didn't "do" anything to your partner and, chances are, it would never occur to her to blame you. Just ask her. And speaking of guilt, don't feel awkward about accepting the **generosity** of friends and family. It is **genuine**. People know how much there is for you both to think about, and if they offer assistance in any way, you can bet they truly want to **give**. Letting friends help is also a **good** way to see them and maintain contact. It will be easy for you and your partner to hide yourselves away with your new baby, forgetting the world outside. Let your friends and family know they are welcome in your new lives. It will give you both perspective and prevent you from getting too obsessive about parent-hood and your new baby.

The two focal points that will **help** you most during expectant fatherhood are as follows: maintain your sense of **humor** and be **honest**. Be sure not to **hide** behind a tough exterior that conceals your true feelings. You may think this is what your partner wants from you, but it's not. While you and your partner may feel **helpless** in the face of any number of situations in these nine months, masking your feelings will only make things **harder**. The truth eventually surfaces, and when it does, you will both wish you had been honest from the beginning. Approaching the events of your pregnancy with truth and laughter will make the process of **handling** them so much easier. Sure, you will be confronted with **hard** issues. But as long as all three of you are **healthy**, you should enjoy your pregnancy.

"Mona and I decided that Wednesday night would be date night, even after the baby was born. We were determined to keep our own relationship fresh and fun, and it worked!"

"It sounds silly, but the day I started fixing up the baby's room was the first time I really felt like an adult."

You have paternal **instincts** just as your partner has maternal ones. You will somehow know certain things about your baby—feel attachments and connections that you don't quite understand. There may be points at which you question these instincts or feel **insecure**, **isolated**, or **irritated**, since our culture and the media do not support a father's role as unconditionally as they do a mother's. Perhaps because you see your partner physically carrying the child you think that parenting is outside your capabilities, that you are not truly **involved** in the pregnancy, or that your role should be secondary. You are wrong. Your baby is part of you and you are part of it. You are a partner in this venture, you have a tremendous role to play with huge **investments** in the process, and your instincts are certainly legitimate. They come from your **intimate** ties to your partner and your baby.

"After Cathy told me we were pregnant I became very anxious and edgy until I realized what a gift fatherhood is to a man. Now I couldn't be more delighted."

You may find yourself **jealous** of your unborn child or of your partner for all of the attention they are receiving. Your role as expectant father may seem thankless from time to time, and you may wish to be recognized for the **job** you are doing, the contributions you are making, and the support you are giving. This is a perfectly **justifiable** sentiment. Instead of getting down on yourself for an honest reaction, or stewing about it and getting angry, let your partner know how you feel and ask her to support you in your role as you are supporting her in hers. Another avenue of encouragement may be your male friends who have children. **Joke** with them. Solicit advice from them. Ask how they felt at times like these and how they dealt with it. They will understand best what you're going through. Above all, it is important to understand that you are not the first or last man to experience these emotions and that they are legitimate.

There are lots of **kid-related** items available. But before you go crazy buying the cutest pair of overalls you've ever seen and the most adorable little straw hat that goes with them, think about your budget. Make a list of what you really need for your baby, and make those purchases first. Ideas for inexpensive yet popular items include brightly-colored **kites**, plastic **keys**, **kaleidoscopes**, or small **keyboards**. Whatever you buy for your child at this stage of life should not require **kid gloves**. Babies can be rough with their toys.

The curriculum of many nursery schools and **kindergartens** is based on a specific methodology of early education. You may want to research Montessori, Waldorf, and other **kinds** of preschools and kindergartens and decide which approach to education you favor. Because of an increase in two-career families, these schools are becoming harder to get into. If you have an idea where you'd like your child to go, you may want to reserve a spot now. Seriously.

"It's not like I'd never expected to be a father, but this was sooner than I had planned. And what a wonderful surprise!"

You may experience increasingly warm and intimate feelings of **love** and **longing** for your partner during the pregnancy. Your pregnancy is an alliance, a shared event, and may draw you closer together. **Listen** to these sentiments and act on them. Keep in mind that your attachment to your child-to-be and your relationship with your partner are closely intertwined. **Labor** will be the point at which this alliance is the most important and the time when all three of you should be together. A father's presence during his baby's delivery is known to alleviate pain and anxiety in expectant mothers, as well as enhance his own experience of his child's birth. Your partner needs to know that she is not alone at such a strenuous time and that there is an end in sight. Your presence is also essential to the effective execution of techniques learned in the **Lamaze** or other prenatal classes you've taken with your partner.

Your partner will have emotional reactions to the physical state of pregnancy and might be quite **moody**. Her hormonal balance is changing, her nutritional needs are more severe, and she must physically adjust to the **mysterious** demands of the baby growing inside her. These changes, coupled with the innumerable anxieties and expectations of pregnancy (including those having to do with **money**) will increase her emotional sensitivity to seemingly harmless issues. Be prepared for these reactions and the fact that you may become moody too. While your hormones are still intact, you have similar anxieties and expectations. Neither of you should discount the other's feelings when such emotions occur. Support one another and let each other know that you are there to share the burdens, no matter what they are. Once your fears are calmed, step outside the situation for a bit. Go to a **movie** or to hear some **music**, and remind yourselves that life is proceeding normally in the outside world. Take advantage of going out, as it will be more difficult to manage after the baby's arrival.

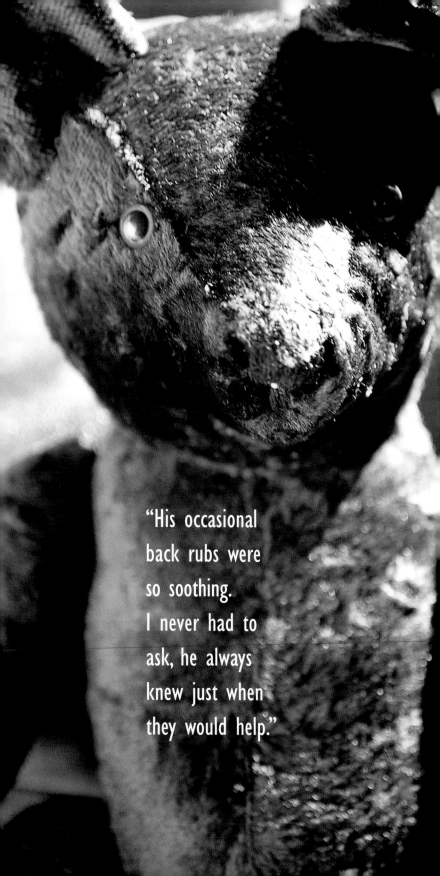

"His occasional
back rubs were
so soothing.
I never had to
ask, he always
knew just when
they would help."

Nausea. She'll feel it. You'll feel it. 'Nuf said.

Your attention to your partner and your baby should not be considered **nagging**; you care and are involved. Your partner needs all the trust, love, and affection you can offer, and it doesn't matter what other people think about your doting. By the same token, your presence in the doctor's office or hospital is not a **nuisance**. Don't let medical staff **neglect** you or your role in the pregnancy. You should attend as many doctor's appointments as possible in order to best understand the medical processes your partner is or will be going through. Being there to understand, listen, and learn is a part of parenthood that has nothing to do with who actually gives birth to the child. This is **nurturing** that you can do as well as your partner.

Make sure that you both feel comfortable with your partner's **obstetrician**. You have an **obligation** to your partner, your baby, and yourself to have a healthy relationship with her doctor, since you all must make decisions together. Her doctor should consider you a full-fledged partner in the pregnancy and include you in all the events to come and issues to be considered. Do not settle for being treated like an **onlooker**. Your involvement, experience, and **observations** during the pregnancy give you a different **outlook** on many of the situations that will arise. This aspect of the pregnancy is very important. If your doctor doesn't recognize this, find another doctor.

Now is the time to **organize** your house and your affairs. There may be plenty of work to do before the baby arrives, from cleaning out the basement and closets to finalizing **outstanding** legal issues. Complicated projects should take place in the early stages of pregnancy, when your partner is less likely to be hampered by the clutter.

Be **prepared**. (See **U: Unprepared**.) Seriously though, this will be the greatest adventure of your life! It is a time for unadulterated **pride**. Revel in your expectant fatherhood in any way you like; just be sure to **participate** on every level of the pregnancy so that you will get the most complete experience. On a **practical** level, finish home and garden **projects** that will be useful to your baby and your partner. As you consider continued participation after your child is born, ask your boss about **paternity** leave.

These nine months will not be without emotional **paradoxes**. For example, you may have feelings of great intimacy concerning the pregnancy coupled with extreme remoteness. Remember that as a **parent** you are also a **person** and that none of us is **perfect**. The best way to deal with these internal conflicts is to **plan** on them arising and voice them to your partner when they do. Be **patient**: it is a virtue that will serve you well for these nine months and in the years to come.

You are no less **qualified** to be a father than your partner is to be a mother. You will become a better father by recognizing that you will have **questions**, **questions**, **questions** along the way and by asking them every chance you get. This is not the time to keep **quiet**. Ask your partner, ask your friends with children, ask your own father, ask your doctor. This is not the time for embarrassment or reservation, so don't be concerned about the **quantity** or **quality** of your **queries**. Afraid your partner will have **quintuplets**? Ask the doctor. Think your expenses will **quadruple** with the birth of your new baby? Ask a friend who's recently become a father. Nothing will get you through this process more easily than honesty, communication, and asking lots of questions. Suppressing your anxieties will only lead to **quarreling**.

As an expectant father, you may have to **rethink** and **redefine** the way you have perceived yourself as an individual in your career, in your **relationships**, and even in your family. Bringing a child into your life demands a certain **reliability** and commitment that may not have been **required** of you before. Remember, though, that you cannot do everything yourself and that you will need **relief** both before and after the baby is born. Friends and family are helpful at these times, offering you opportunities to **relax** and **rejuvenate**.

Your new **role** as husband and father demands that you be **resourceful. Run** errands that your partner is too tired to run. If you haven't done much of the cooking in the house, start now. **Repair** the walkway in the front yard, **restore** the old rocking chair, or **refinish** the chest in the corner. You may be too busy to do these jobs once the baby arrives.

Start making your house **safe** for your child. Child-proofing mechanisms should be installed on cabinets and doors to prevent a curious child from getting access to anything dangerous. Remove poisonous plants from a child's reach, put barriers in front of stairs, and plug up any unused electrical outlets.

You may meet with opposition to your commitment to the pregnancy from people **stuck** in a time when fathers were not as involved in their partner's pregnancies. Don't let them convince you that you are not of the utmost **significance** during this time. Your feelings of positive **self-worth** regarding your fatherhood will not only contribute to a healthy, couple-focused pregnancy, but will counteract any alienation or discouragement. If you do not want to take a **secondary** role in your pregnancy, you must **stand** up to criticism and be willing to **share** the responsibility. You will have to give up a certain **self-centeredness** that you may not have known you had: **sports car** or **station wagon**—you'll make the right decision.

"I thought I would be able to work right up to the birth, but after my second trimester the doctor told me I had to stop."

"It was tough financially, but we made it. The difficulty has made us more focused; our priorities sorted themselves out right away."

"Joe and I love taking weekend trips. Maybe we won't be as adventuresome, but we are already thinking of ways to make quick, easy trips away from the city with the baby."

Be **truthful** and honest with yourself and your partner. Try not to do anything you don't want to do or be anything you aren't because of what you think is expected of you. Such self-betrayal will ultimately have negative effects, as you become resentful for having to act in a way that is not sincere. **Trust** your own emotions, reactions, and contributions. Don't pressure yourself (or let anyone else pressure you) to be calm, cool, and collected if you don't feel that way. **Tell** others what is difficult for you and what would make things less difficult. If you get nervous at the doctor's office, don't make up excuses not to go. Explain your fears to your partner. You are in this pregnancy **together**, and she should be helping you through the **tough times** just as you are helping her. **Talk** to your unborn child. Studies have shown that infants recognize and respond to the voices they heard while in the womb.

Be prepared to be completely **unprepared** for what you are about to experience. Unless you have been through a pregnancy before, there is no way to predict the range and extremity of situations and emotions that you are about to experience. Don't be **uninvolved** out of fear. Take solace in knowing that you are not alone, that men before you have been where you are now, that others will be there in the future, and that the outcome of this pregnancy will be more fulfilling than you could ever imagine. Read helpful literature and ask questions. The more involved you are and the more informed you become, the more you will **understand** and the better prepared you will be to deal with anything that comes your way. In this way, you begin building the foundation of a **unified** family.

Spend time **visiting** friends and family during the pregnancy. Once the baby arrives, it may be a while before you will have time to see friends or to entertain them in your home. Remind your friends and family that while you will be busy once the baby comes, you don't want to lose touch with them, and they should not be afraid to call you. You will be thankful for contact with the outside world!

Your handling of the pregnancy adds to the family **values** that will last your child's lifetime. In this way, your positive support, involvement, contribution, and education is **vital**. Don't stop thinking ahead and planning once your child arrives. You have a lifetime of events to look forward to—from first words, first steps, and first day of school to first car and high school prom. If planning and preparing has made you feel **valuable** during the pregnancy, it will continue to make you feel so throughout your child's life. So fix up that old car in the garage for your daughter or son. There's no rush, of course—you've got sixteen years!

Building a family is hard **work**, but it is one of the most gratifying endeavors you will ever pursue. Keep in mind that not everyone is skilled at the same kinds of tasks. Don't force yourself to make contributions you are uncomfortable with simply because that's what a father is "supposed to do." Do the work that you do well and you are guaranteed a fulfilling contribution to your pregnancy. If you're not a cook, don't force yourself into the kitchen. Offer to do the food shopping or to pick up some take-out for the two of you. If you are not interested in yard work but you are a fine carpenter, hire a gardener for the garden and build a crib or rocking horse for your baby. Focus on contributions that make you feel good. Of course, the work you do should be tempered with time to reflect. Let the magic and **wonder** of the pregnancy amaze and inspire you. Share your experiences with your partner, and you both will be enriched. Remember that asking questions and expressing your emotions—whether joys or fears—is not a sign of **weakness** but a sign of the **worth** you place on yourself, your partner, and your baby.

Expectant fatherhood can become your own personal **Xanadu**. You will need to take **x-tra** time just to relax and retreat from the flurry of activity that will arrive with your baby. Take advantage of the time afforded by the pregnancy to plan for your baby, speculate on your future as a father, and celebrate the growth of your family. You and your partner have lots to fantasize about concerning your new baby. What will **Xmas** be like with a child in the house? What do you think your child's first word will be? Imagine the wonderful games you will teach your child to play; the great feats your child will perform. Will you have a girl (two **x-chromosomes**) or a boy (one X- and one Y-chromosome)? Think about sitting in a chair, reading aloud with your child on your lap. What music will you play around your baby? There is so much to be **x-cited** about and no reason to hold back.

"I may not be able to control all
the events in my life, but fatherhood
has taught me how to control my
attitude about those events."

"It all works out somehow.
It just all works out."

You may occasionally think that once your child arrives you will **yearn** for the days of **yesteryear** when the **yoke** of parenthood was not strapped to your shoulders. You may think that the money you will spend on your child could have bought you the **yacht** you'd always wanted, or that the time you spend with your crying baby would be better spent in the **yard** or garage. This is an understandable anxiety, and one that your partner probably shares. But this is not what being a parent is about, and you know it. It would be a lie to claim that each moment of your life with your new child will be blissful, but even the smallest joys with your baby will make the sacrifices and difficult times easy to accept.

For many men, fatherhood makes them feel like **Zeus** at the peak of their lives. Unlike career peaks, which come and go, the peak that you attain through fatherhood will last your lifetime. The **zest** for living you feel as a brand-new parent will last forever. From buying your baby a stuffed **zebra** toy to taking a trip to the **zoo** years later to see the real thing, the joy and wonder that your child experiences will become your own. In the early years, bask in the excitement of your child's understanding that a **zipper** goes up and down. In the college years, learn with them as they study the teachings of **Zen** Buddhism. There will be a **zillion** points of joy, wonder, disappointment, success, and failure in your child's life, and you don't want to miss any opportunity to share, congratulate, console, or support. Whatever path your child chooses to take, take it together—you are both guaranteed to live more fully.

9 8 7 6 5 4 3 2 1

Digit on the right indicates the number of this printing.

Library of Congress Catalog Card Number: 96-71144

ISBN 0-7624-0192-3

This book was compiled, designed, and produced by
  Marquand Books, Inc.
  1402 Third Avenue, Suite 300
  Seattle, WA 98101

Edited by Greg Jones

This book may be ordered by mail from the publishers. Please include $2.50 for postage and handling. *But try your bookstore first!*
  Running Press Book Publishers
  125 South Twenty-second Street
  Philadelphia, Pennsylvania 19103-4399

Printed in Hong Kong

THE NEW HARTFORD MEMORIAL LIBRARY
P.O. Box 247
Central Avenue at Town Hill Road
New Hartford, Connecticut 06057
(860) 379-7235

THE STORY OF
HARRIET TUBMAN

FREEDOM TRAIN

by Dorothy Sterling

SCHOLASTIC INC.
New York Toronto London Auckland Sydney

*For my daughter, so that she may know
the story of a great American woman.*

ISBN 0-590-40640-X

12 11 10 9 8 7 6   8 9/8 0 1 2/9

CONTENTS

Little Girl, Little Girl!

Harriet sat in the middle of the floor with the baby in her arms. Her thin body swayed from side to side as she tried to quiet him.

> Hushaby
> Don't you cry.
> Go to sleep, little baby,

she crooned. Slowly his eyes blinked closed and his tiny head dropped back on her shoulder.

Harriet stopped rocking. "Hope you're asleep now for good and sure," she scolded. "You done me in all right this morning." Raising her eyes from his face, flushed and fretful even in sleep, she stretched her aching neck. Then she leaned back until she could look out of the window.

5

Outside a light spring breeze rippled the pink-and-white magnolia blossoms. A mockingbird flew to the stately oak which shaded the gateway of the Big House. In the distance, Harriet could see the tops of scrubby pines growing out of the salt marshes along the Bay. As she watched, a flock of geese rose above the pines. Fanning out behind their leader in V formation, they headed northward.

The sky stretched blue and cloudless, and the sun was dazzling on the tops of the trees. When she closed her eyes, she could picture the green velvet of the Big House lawns, sloping down to neat fence rows. She could hear the honking of the geese and the sweet trill of the mockingbird, and a murmur of song and talk from the workers in the fields. That would be her brothers setting out the young tobacco plants and her mother hilling up the soil around the corn or straightening the rows of yellow wheat. Far off in the woods, Daddy Ben was cutting down oak trees for the Baltimore shipyards. Harriet imagined she could hear the ringing impact of his ax and smell the fresh, clean smell of the newly fallen trees.

After the cold of winter and the long spring rains, everything was green and alive. Today was a day for running and skipping, for rolling on the grass; a day for climbing trees and hunting frogs' eggs in the swamp. It was a day for singing with the birds.

But the year was 1827 and the place, Maryland. Harriet, black-haired and black-skinned, was a slave, the daughter of a slave, the granddaughter of a slave. A hundred years before, the captain of a sailing vessel had kidnaped her great-grandmother. Carrying her across the ocean from her African home to a crowded wharf in Baltimore, he sold her to the highest bidder. Now her children and her children's children and their children belonged to Master, as surely as did his cows and pigs.

Although Harriet had not yet passed her eighth birthday, there was no running and skipping for her, no rolling on the grass or climbing in the trees. For her there was only work, and sometimes a stolen minute to look through the window and watch the birds as they flew North.

North. The word brought her from the sunny world outside to the room in which she sat with the sleeping baby in her lap. North. Some said it was bitter cold there and that the people — Yankees, they called them — all had horns. Others said that everyone in the North was free, black and white alike. School for all the children, no masters, no whippings.

"Sounds like the heaven Old Cudjoe's always talking about," Harriet whispered to herself. "Wonder what it's really like."

She counted up what she had done that morning

and yesterday morning, and what she would do to-morrow. Up before the sun to light the fires. Sweeping, dusting, rocking the baby while Miss Sarah breakfasted. When Mistress got back from shopping, Harriet would be sent to the kitchen to peel potatoes and pluck chickens for lunch. Then more washing, more cleaning, more soothing the fretful baby. Even when he was put to bed for the night, she must sit beside him in the dark, rocking his cradle when he cried, lest he disturb his mother's rest.

The baby whimpered. Softly Harriet sang to him one of the slave children's songs:

> Little girl, little girl!
> Did you go to the spring?
> Yes ma'am!
> Did you feed my ducks?
> Did my ducks lay eggs?
> Yes ma'am! Yes ma'am!
> Did you take um to the house?
> Did you bake some bread?
> Yes ma'am! Yes ma'am!
> Did the bread taste good?
> Yes ma'am! Yes ma'am!

As he quieted again, she thought about last year when she had been too little for the Big House. Then she brought water to the men and women in the fields, and sped barefoot from one end of the great

plantation to the other to carry messages from Master to the overseers. On hot summer days she had crawled along the rows of tobacco plants with the other children, picking fat green hornworms from the underside of the shiny leaves. At harvesttime, when all hands, large and small, were busy, she had shucked corn, sometimes working beside her parents until late at night.

But there had been days of no work at all, when she waded in the creek, hunting for crabs, or followed Daddy Ben's crew to the woods. Once, one wonderful time, she sailed all the way up the Bay to Baltimore with Daddy Ben, to deliver a load of logs to the shipyard. Then she had seen a city such as she had never dreamed of — rows and rows of houses with white stone steps, and cobblestoned streets and a great bridge across the river.

It was after the trip to Baltimore that Master had spoken to her mother. "Noticed her on the boat," he'd said to Old Rit. "Seems little and skinny, but she'll fill out. Can't rightly keep track of the ages of all the black babies around here. Registering the colts and calves is enough trouble," he'd laughed. "But she looks old enough to be of some use."

The next day Miss Sarah came to the cabin with a new cotton shift, to replace the torn flour sacking which was Harriet's only clothing. When she had

dressed, Miss Sarah took her in the carriage for a drive to Bucktown. Before Harriet realized what was happening, she found herself at the home of James Cook, whose wife was a weaver.

"After Mrs. Cook has taught you to weave, you can come back home and work on our looms," Miss Sarah said when she left. "But mind now, you'd better be a good girl."

Desperately lonely for Old Rit and Daddy Ben and her brothers and sister, Harriet tried hard to be good. But nothing seemed to go right at the Cooks. By the time she had scrubbed floors and pounded out the wash, her stubby fingers were too tired to follow her mistress' instructions at the loom.

"Stupid girl," Mrs. Cook kept telling her. "Stupid girl." Mr. Cook agreed when, impatient with her awkwardness, his wife turned Harriet over to him for outdoor chores.

Then came the day when Harriet fell sick. There were bumps all over her body, and her head ached. Paying no attention to her complaints, Mr. Cook took her with him to the marshes to watch his muskrat traps. She stumbled along, tripping on hummocks of swamp grass, barely able to see for the pain in her head. Finally she fell in the low water and could not get up.

That was all she remembered until she found her-

self at home again, with Old Rit putting wet leaves on her burning skin.

"It's all right, honey," her mother comforted her. "Mr. Cook brought you back yesterday. Said you weren't worth the salt to season your food. You've got the measles. Mistress promised I can take care of you until you're well again."

When the last measles spot had disappeared, Miss Sarah called her to the Big House. "You're going to work here now," she told her, "and this time, no non-sense."

"No nonsense," Harriet brooded. "Means washing and sweeping and always the baby crying. And never a friendly word. Sometimes I think I can't stand it no longer.

"No nonsense, baby," she told him fiercely. "Hear that now? No nonsense."

As her voice sounded in the empty room, the baby's head rolled forward. His eyes and mouth opened wide. Before he could get out his cry, Harriet tried to quiet him with a song:

> Juber do and Juber don't
> Juber will and Juber won't
> Juber up and Juber down
> Juber all around the town.

Her voice rang out, firm and sweet, but the baby refused to be comforted. The louder he cried, the

faster Harriet rocked and the more vigorously she
sang:

> Sift the meal and gimme the husk
> Bake the cake and gimme the crust
> Fry the pork and gimme the skin.
> Ask me when I'm coming again.
> Juber, Juber, Juber-ee.

Downstairs, the front door slammed closed, and
Miss Sarah's footsteps echoed in the hall. Wildly Harriet rocked and wildly the baby cried.

"Now I'm gonna catch it," she told the baby.
"Trouble with both of us is that we're hungry. Here
your mammy comes to feed you, but that ain't going to help me much."

Mistress burst into the room. "Hand me the child!"
she ordered. "Why did you let him cry? You know
what the doctor said."

Harriet's eyelids drooped to hide her bright eyes.
Her lips protruded and her face took on a sullen, va-
cant expression which had not been there a moment
before. She struggled to get up, but the baby was
too heavy for her. As Mistress took him from her
arms, she automatically dodged the blow which she
knew would come. Only then did she attempt to speak
in her own defense.

"Baby slept all morning," she muttered. "Only
wake just now 'cause he was hungry."

Ignoring her explanation, Miss Sarah sent her to the kitchen. She helped Cook get ready for lunch and then followed Fred, butler of the Big House, when he carried the steaming platters to the dining table. During the meal she stood next to Miss Sarah, fetching salt and butter, and running to the kitchen when something more was needed.

The smell of the food made Harriet's nostrils quiver. She had breakfasted on hoecake browned in the kitchen fireplace. For lunch, if there was time, she would be given hoecake again, for supper salt pork. She was everlastingly hungry, everlastingly sick of the corn meal and pork, corn meal and pork, which was her daily ration. There were nights when she dreamed of good things to eat, of platters of chicken and brown gravy, of frosted cakes and mounds of candy.

Her eyes fastened on the silver sugar bowl at Mistress' elbow. She stared at the bowl, fascinated, while Master and Mistress engaged in angry argument. Slowly she moved toward it, scarcely hearing their shouted words. Now her fingers were only a few inches from a precious lump. Now they were dipping into the bowl. But before they could pick up the sugar, Miss Sarah turned.

"Harriet!" she screamed. This time she would not be satisfied with a careless cuff. "Make the little slaves

mind you or flog them," she always said. Pushing back her chair, she strode to the fireplace, where a rawhide whip hung next to the mantelpiece.

Without thinking of what she was doing, Harriet made for the door. Three jumps and she was down the steps and out of the house. Up the road she flew, listening anxiously for the sound of pursuers. Faster and faster she ran, past the overseer's house, past the slave cabins, never daring to stop. Always behind her were the footsteps of Master and the shouted calls of Miss Sarah.

Finally, when it seemed as if there was no breath left in her body, she came to a big pigpen. There was an old sow there and eight little pigs. Unable to climb the fence, she wriggled through the bars and threw herself onto the muddy ground. As she lay there, with the sow nosing her face, she could hear Master and Mistress on the road, angrily calling her name.

Until it was dark, she didn't dare to move. Then she crawled to the trough where the pigs' food was placed, and fought with the little pigs for a share of potato peelings and scraps of meat. Fearful of the sow, who kept pushing her away, she made a bed of muddy straw for herself in the far corner of the pen. Hungry, cold, and miserable, she finally fell asleep.

All that night and all the next day Harriet hid in

the pigpen, afraid of the sow, but more afraid of Miss Sarah. When the pigs slept, she scraped the trough for food. When they woke, she rolled back to her straw bed. After dark she lay awake, staring at the cold, bright light of the stars and wondering what she should do.

A row of stars pointed to one which Harriet knew. Each night, when the other stars moved across the sky in steady procession, Harriet's star stood still. Winter and summer, at dusk and at dawn, it was always in the same place. To her it seemed as if the whole sky revolved around it.

Watching it, she remembered talk she had overheard about the free land to which this star could lead. For the first time since she had run away, she began to cry. As her body shook with sobs, she felt a gentle hand on her shoulder, heard a soft voice close to her ear.

"Harriet," the voice whispered. "It's me, Daddy Ben. Don't cry, honey. I been looking for you since yesterday afternoon. Ever since Fred told me what happened."

Strong arms lifted the shaking child. Tenderly Ben wrapped his ragged cotton shirt around her bare shoulders.

"You shouldn'a done it," he softly reproached her. "You got yourself a peck of trouble. Ma and I will

do our best to get you out of it, but you know we can't help much."

Harriet was quiet, content to lie back in her father's arms and feel his warm body close to hers. For a moment she felt safe. Then, as he lifted her over the bars of the pen, taking her from the pigs' world to the world of people again, she had a question for him.

"Daddy Ben, what do they call that star — the one that never moves?" She pointed with her finger.

Ben bent his head and kissed her forehead. "That's the North Star, child. The best star there is. But you mustn't be thinking about that now — not yet."

Peck of Trouble

HARRIET SLEPT THAT NIGHT and all the next day in her parents' cabin. It was a restless sleep, broken by nightmares of angry white faces. Over and over again she dreamed of children marching along a dusty road, their wrists and ankles linked to a long rope. It was thus that she had last seen her two older sisters, who had been taken from their home and sold to the Deep South to work in the cotton fields.

Awakening late in the afternoon, she was still too tired to get up. The windowless cabin was dark in the daytime, but a few slanting rays of sunshine found their way in through the cracks in the log walls, making a crazy pattern on the bare earth floor.

From the door, hanging crookedly on its hinges, a patch of light shone on the fireplace. With its chimney of split sticks plastered with mud, the fireplace was the heart of the cabin, the source of heat and light and food. Neatly stacked on the hearth was an assortment of pots and pails. On one side was the potato hole, covered with boards, where sweet potatoes kept firm and hard all winter long. On the other were two backless, battered chairs.

Straw pallets lined the log walls. These were the beds for Benjamin and William Henry and Mary Ann, who still slept at home with their parents. Harriet's other brothers, James, Henry, Robert, and John, lived with their wives in cabins in the quarters or were hired out to work on neighboring plantations. They were permitted to come home each Christmas to visit their family.

The children's beds were covered with torn rags, but Rit and Daddy Ben's was spread with a glowing patchwork quilt of green and brown and yellow cloth. Harriet's eyes lit up when she looked at the quilt.

She could remember her mother starting it when Benjie was a baby. Rit had patiently collected discarded bits of material, torn dresses, and fragments of men's suits from the Big House. Each scrap was scrubbed and hung on the bushes to bleach in the

sun. Then the prettiest colors were chosen for the cover and the rest for stuffing. Rit worked on it late at night by the light of the fire, until she finally completed it last winter in time for Christmas.

It was warm and soft and colorful, the household's only treasure. "When I grow up," Harriet always promised herself, "I'm going to make one exactly like it."

In the distance a blast from the overseer's horn signaled the end of the working day. Benjamin and William Henry were the first to swing back the door, eager to hear of Harriet's adventures. Mary Ann, who worked as a chambermaid in the Big House, often didn't come home until late at night. Old Rit bustled in after the boys, worried about her daughter and full of household problems.

"Here you, Benjie," she fussed, "take the pail and go down to the spring for water. And mind you wash your hands while you're there. William Henry, I told you this morning to fetch some wood for the fire. You go right out and get me an armful, or there won't be supper for any of you tonight."

After the weary boys had trudged out, she sat down next to Harriet and stroked her curly black hair. "You showed right bad sense," she gently scolded. "I'm afraid for you."

Harriet threw her arms around her mother's neck,

and for a moment there were tears on both their faces. "Do they know I'm here yet?" the little girl whispered.

"No." Old Rit shook her head. "But they been down the last two nights looking for you. They'll find you right enough."

The hinges of the door creaked. Anxiously Harriet and her mother looked to see who was coming in. It was Ben, the sweat running down his dark face and a sack bobbing on his back. He was not a tall man, but his broad shoulders and powerful arms seemed to fill up the cabin.

"Where the boys?" he asked. "Got a muskrat here for supper."

Muskrats thrived in the swamps along the Bay, and their skins brought good money in the Cambridge and Baltimore markets. But all muskrats belonged to Master, and it was worth thirty lashes for any slave caught trapping and eating one.

"More trouble." Rit shook her head despairingly.

"Nobody saw me," Ben cheerfully insisted. "This child needs fattening up. Can't fill her stomach without real meat sometimes."

Before Ben had finished skinning the muskrat, Benjie and William Henry burst in, loaded down with wood and water. A blazing fire of pine knots soon filled the room with its warm white light, and cooking smells mingled with the sweet, resinous

odor of the burning wood. Sitting cross-legged on the hearth, Harriet watched her mother stir batter for corn bread. If only she could stay home like this always, with Old Rit and Daddy Ben and the boys.

It was long after dark when the family finished supper. The boys' heads were nodding, and the fire had burned down to a mass of red coals. Not until then did Ben put his arm around Harriet's shoulders and tell her of his talk with Master.

"I went right up to him when he come to the woods this afternoon and asked him to let you be. Told him he should whip me instead. But he says Miss Sarah is fit to be tied. She never did like you since you took sick at the Cooks. Says you'll grow up to be a troublemaker. She's talking of selling you South."

A thin whimper escaped from Harriet's lips.

"But it's not as bad as all that, honey," Ben comforted her. "Seeing as how I'm a valuable property — worth five dollars a day to him any time he wants to hire me out — he'll keep you here. But Miss Sarah's set to flog you, to make an example for the other children."

"Don't care what she do to me" — Harriet's voice was unsteady — "so long as she don't sell me away from you. But will I have to go back to the Big House to work for her?"

"No." Ben shook his head. "Mistress say she's

given up trying to make a house servant out of you. All you're good for is to work in the fields."

Now Old Rit interrupted, her voice rough and angry, the way it was when she was upset. "Didn't want you to be a field hand like me," she mourned. "Work in the house, sometimes you get to sit down. There's food from the kitchen and the ladies' old clothes to wear. Work in the fields, it's from sunup to sundown. And half the time not enough to eat or a pair of shoes in winter. Mary Ann, she learned to smile at Mistress and say 'Yes ma'am' and 'No ma'am.' But you won't even try. Since you been a baby, I keep telling you, 'Smile at the white folks.'"

"But I don't care, Ma," Harriet tried to comfort Old Rit. "The Big House is maybe all right for Mary Ann, but not for me. Something inside me won't let me smile at Mistress. When she talks to me, I feel all hard inside, like I swallowed a stone."

Ben took his daughter's side. "Can't smile always, Rit. I been working all my life with my mouth shut. Since I been as big as Benjie here, Master's promised me freedom if I was a good boy. But it's always 'some day,' like the Day of Jubilee. Don't expect now I'll be free 'fore I get to heaven. Harriet can't help the way she is. Maybe her way's better than ours."

With the hardness inside her, Harriet followed Ben to the Big House next morning. The whip cut

into her bare thin back until it seemed as if her shoulder blades would crack under it. But she set her jaw and refused to cry out. When it was over, she was shoved to the door to find her way home as best she could.

Half walking, half crawling, she stumbled to the cabin. Hours later her mother found her lying on the floor just inside the door. Lifting her to a bed, she greased the torn back with lard, then gently covered her with the patchwork quilt.

"Good-bye for now," Old Rit whispered. "Got to get back to my hoeing before old overseer catch me."

The pain was bad, worse than anything Harriet had ever known before. Every part of her body felt bruised and cut. Her lips were parched, and she ached for water. But when she tried to crawl to the hearth for the drinking pail, her head seemed to float away.

After a while a soft breeze came in through the half-opened door and cooled her burning skin. Clutching the patchwork quilt, she fell asleep. Again she dreamed. But this time her dreams were of deep woods and wide rivers. And always in front of her was a shining star to guide her.

School Days

As soon as Harriet was able to walk again, she was sent to the fields. There Benjie and William Henry showed her how to sucker the broad-leaved tobacco plants and, with a hickory-handled hoe that was taller than she, to chop down the weeds around the corn. When harvesttime came she cut hay and stacked dried cornstalks, or drove an oxcart laden with hogsheads of tobacco to the market in Cambridge. In the winter there was wood to be split and hauled for the fireplaces in the Big House. Early in the spring, when the geese were flying North, she learned to guide a wooden plow across the flat meadows by the Bay, the reins of the mule securely tied around her small waist.

The days were long and the tasks were hard. "We work from can to can't," the older women grumbled. Harriet's head nodded over her supper each night, and she fell into a deep and dreamless sleep as soon as she stretched out on her pallet.

But slave children grew up quickly in Maryland in the 1820's. The weak who dropped exhausted in the fields were comforted with the overseer's lash and the threat of sale to the cotton planters. Only the strong survived.

Gradually the blisters on Harriet's hands changed to calluses, and the muscles in her arms grew round and firm. As she worked in the sun, side by side with her own people, she gained strength in spirit as well as in body. Joining her voice with the birds, she brought down her hoe or clacked her reins to the rhythm of a song, half nonsense, half rich with meaning:

> The Jack Snipe said unto the Crane
> "I wish to the Lord there would come rain."
> The wild Goose said unto the Swan,
> "The coming winter'll be sharp and long."
>
> They say old Marse is sick again.
> He suffer many a' ache and pain.
> When my old Marse's dead and gone
> This old slave'll stop husking corn.

Or, in another mood, she turned to one of the spir-

ituals which Negroes all over the South were composing:

> There's no rain to wet you,
> Oh yes, I want to go home.
> There's no sun to burn you,
> Oh yes, I want to go home.
> Oh, push along, believers,
> Oh yes, I want to go home.
> There's no whips a-cracking,
> Oh yes, I want to go home.
> My brother on the wayside,
> Oh yes, I want to go home.
> Oh push along, my brother,
> Oh yes, I want to go home.
> Where there's no stormy weather,
> Oh yes, I want to go home.
> There's no tribulation,
> Oh yes, I want to go home.

As they listened to her sweet contralto, her neighbors' faces sobered and their hoes hacked at the weeds with sudden fierceness. There was not a man or woman in the fields who didn't dream of the heaven they had heard of from the Bible. But Harriet's voice, young and confident, gave them hope of "no whips a-cracking" not only in the hereafter but in the here-and-now.

Singing, Harriet learned, was something like smiling. The white folks wanted the slaves to sing. A si-

lent slave might mean a discontented slave, plotting rebellion or escape. Often when the rows of tired workers grew silent or there was whispering along the line, the overseer would leap from his post on the fence rail and shout, "Make a noise there! Make a noise there! Sing up!"

If he wanted singing, Harriet would give it to him. But never meekly. The songs she chose and her defiant manner worried Old Rit. Anxiously she watched Harriet toss her head back and sing of men of another day who had been enslaved but had found freedom:

> Didn't my Lord deliver Daniel,
> Deliver Daniel, deliver Daniel?
> Didn't my Lord deliver Daniel,
> And why not every man?

Following her lead, Benjie or William Henry took up the verse:

> He delivered Daniel from the lion's den,
> Jonah from the belly of the whale.
> And the Hebrew children
> From the fiery furnace.

Before the overseer's long strides had carried him back to the fence, a chorus of voices demanded to know:

"Why not every man?"

The Bible was the slaves' storybook and the source of hope and inspiration for their songs. Young and old gathered together under the spreading branches of the oak tree at the edge of the woods each Sunday morning to hear the tales of the children of Israel, whose oppression seemed so much like their own. As far back as Harriet could remember, Old Cudjoe had told them of the Jews' long fight for freedom. Youngsters sat openmouthed as he described the plagues and pestilences with which God had punished the Egyptian slaveholders.

"And it came to pass," Old Cudjoe thundered, "that the Lord killed all the first-born in that land of Egypt, from King Pharaoh to the prisoners in jail.

"And Moses led his people out of Egypt into the wilderness," he continued. "The children of Israel were sore afraid because Old Pharaoh chased after them with chariots and horsemen. But God held back the water of the sea to let Moses pass. Then he caused the water to rise again and drown all Pharaoh's army."

There were murmurs of "Amen!" Then the group burst into song:

> Go down, Moses,
> Way down in Egypt's land.
> Tell ole Pharaoh,
> Let my people go.

This was the part Harriet liked best. Her small body swayed and her eyes shone as verse followed verse:

> When Israel was in Egypt's land,
> Let my people go.
> Oppressed so hard they could not stand,
> Let my people go.
>
> No more shall they in bondage toil,
> Let my people go.
> Let them come out with Egypt's spoil,
> Let my people go.

Cudjoe was the oldest man on the plantation — "older than sin," he used to say. He had been born on the slave ship which carried his mother from the coast of Africa. When she died during her first American winter, Old Mistress, Miss Sarah's mother, took a fancy to the tiny black baby. Bringing him up with her own children, she had even allowed him to learn to read and write.

He remembered the Indian raids and the War of the Revolution, when, side by side with his master, he had shouldered a musket and fought the British King. To the slaves at home he brought back news of a paper that Franklin and Jefferson and Adams signed in Philadelphia.

"Says all men are equal and have the same right to life, liberty, and happiness," he explained as the Negroes crowded into his little cabin.

For the next few years he had continued to assure them that their day of liberation was not far away. One by one, each state in the North forbade slavery within its borders. In Haiti, the West Indian island where Columbus first planted the Spanish flag, Negroes revolted against their masters and set up a free republic. Slavery was abolished in Mexico, in South America, in all the colonies belonging to the British Crown.

But cotton prices soared and the northern merchants bid feverishly for the tobacco and farm produce of Maryland and Virginia. Bitterly Old Cudjoe realized that the plantation owners would never willingly free the men and women who cultivated their lands. Now he acted as teacher to the younger slaves, passing on to them the scraps of information he could gather about the fight for their liberation.

News came to him quickly over the grapevine telegraph. This was a remarkable invention which required no receiving or sending apparatus. It depended on sharp ears and bright eyes and bare feet which knew how to run swiftly but silently. All the slaves on the Eastern Shore — the house servants, the field hands, the boys who drove their masters to town twice each week for the mail — worked for the grapevine telegraph.

If Mr. Stewart's boy, Thomas, took to his heels one

dark night and followed the rivers north to Pennsylvania and freedom, Cudjoe was sure to know it by cock's crow the next day. If dinner guests at the Thompsons' brought reports of a slave uprising in South Carolina or, warmed with wine and good food, damned "those Yankee Abolitionists" who wanted to do away with slavery, Cudjoe spread their words a few hours later. Were there slave traders in Cambridge shopping for likely field hands, or rewards posted for runaways, the news reached Cudjoe's cabin before it did the Big House.

Magazines and newspapers had a way of traveling from Master's library to Cudjoe's. Late at night, by the bright light of the pine knots in his fireplace, he studied them. When his neighbors slipped in he would read aloud, slowly tracing each word with his forefinger.

It was at the end of Harriet's second year in the fields that Old Cudjoe read David Walker's *Appeal*. Walker was a free Negro, born in North Carolina, but now working and writing in Boston. Struggling to keep awake, Harriet listened to Cudjoe's deep voice: "Are we men? I ask you . . . Are we MEN? . . . America is more our country than it is the whites' — we have enriched it with our blood and tears. The greatest riches in all America have arisen from our blood and tears."

Only a few months later, he told them of a white man who had come from New England to publish a paper in Baltimore, just fifty miles up the Bay. Young William Lloyd Garrison had been thrown in jail for daring to criticize shipowners who carried slave cargoes down the coast to New Orleans.

That a white man was willing to give up his own freedom in a fight for black men was a startling idea. Harriet puzzled over it for a long time.

"There's hundreds like that in the North," Old Cudjoe assured her. "Women too. Writing papers, making speeches, saying we should be freed. Even right here in Maryland there's Quakers who think owning another man is a sin against God."

"You think maybe they'll get us free sometime?" Harriet wondered.

"They — and us," Cudjoe replied. "Up in Philadelphia, I read, black men been having meetings too, to talk about ending slavery. Don't figure on angels of the Lord flying here waving fiery swords at Master. We got to do things ourselves. Then, with the help of the Lord and the Abolitionists, we're sure to make it."

One hot August morning, when Harriet was eleven, the grapevine telegraph buzzed with news. Children with water buckets carried the word from the Big House. Bent heads in the fields whispered it along

the rows. When the overseer's back was turned, Harriet slipped away to tell Daddy Ben's crew in the woods.

Across the state line in Virginia, a slave named Nat Turner and five of his friends had armed themselves and killed their master. Traveling from plantation to plantation, they were freeing Negroes and shooting slaveowners, sparing only the poor whites who owned no slaves. By noon that day, an army of seventy freed men with a small arsenal of axes and guns was on the march.

Harriet began to calculate how long it would take Nat Turner to reach the Eastern Shore of Maryland. "If they get boats and sail across the Bay," she whispered to William Henry, "I figure they could be here in a week's time."

Late that night Fred came running from the Big House. Breathlessly he told how a thousand soldiers called up by the Governor had stopped Nat Turner's army.

"They're shooting them and hanging them, a dozen at a time." His voice broke. "But they haven't catched Nat Turner."

Wide-eyed, Harriet listened. They hadn't caught Nat Turner yet. The rebellion had been stopped, but its leader was still free. There was still some hope, one small desperate chance, that he would make his way

across the Chesapeake to lead the slaves of Maryland. Day after day she listened to the whispers.

"Haven't catched old Nat yet."

"Never will catch old Nat."

More than two months went by before a patroller, passing a clearing in the woods, saw a black man emerge from a hole in the ground. Then the slave-owners' justice was swift and sure, and Nat Turner went defiantly to his death on the gallows.

The revolt in Virginia terrified Master and Mistress. "Afraid they'll wake up one morning and find we've all run off," Fred reported. "Master and Mr. Thompson and the others had a meeting. They're hiring patrollers to ride the roads every night. Got a special pack of dogs that's trained to go after anyone with a black skin."

All through the South, old slave laws were strengthened and new ones passed. Negroes were forbidden to blow horns or beat drums, or to meet together without a white man present. The Bible was outlawed in the slave quarters, and the penalty for teaching a slave to read was life imprisonment or death. No slave could set his foot on the highway, even on Master's business, without a written pass explaining where he was going and when he would return. There was a watchman stationed at every gate, a guard at every ferry, a sentinel at every bridge.

From a smuggled newspaper, Old Cudjoe read of a speech in the Virginia legislature. "We have as far as possible closed every avenue by which light may enter slaves' minds," a delegate declaimed. "If we could extinguish the capacity to see the light, our work would be completed; they would then be on a level with the beasts of the field."

But it was not easy to destroy the capacity to see the light. At Christmastime, six weeks after Nat Turner's death, Cudjoe was called to the Big House. Returning to the quarters with a drawn face, he sought out Daddy Ben.

"Master says no more of our own Sunday school or church. We get forty lashes for singing songs like 'Go Down Moses.' "

"Did you talk up to him?" Ben asked.

Cudjoe nodded. "Told him our children has souls just like his. He's gonna get us a white preacher once a month. Next spring he'll drive us to Cambridge for one of those revival meetings."

The white preacher came, Sunday after Sunday, to read carefully selected texts from the Bible. "Servants, be obedient to them that are your masters," he would preach. "Blessed are the meek: for they shall inherit the earth."

"He tell us God's got a clean kitchen to put us in when we get to heaven," Old Rit grumbled. "And

you know, sure enough, who's going to keep it clean. Us black angels." And suddenly there was laughter.

Gradually the attendance at the meetings under the oak tree dwindled. In their place came secret gatherings in the forest. When the moon was on the wane, Cudjoe lifted his hoe and sang:

> Steal away, steal away
> Steal away to Jesus.
> Steal away, steal away home.

Everyone joined in to show that they understood the signal:

> I ain't got long to stay here.
> My Lord he calls me.
> He calls me by the thunder.
> The trumpet sounds within my soul.
> I ain't got long to stay here.
> Steal away home.

Swinging his legs and nodding his head to the peaceful rhythm of the hymn, the overseer smiled. "No trouble here," he assured himself.

Harriet and Benjie could hardly keep from laughing. They knew that as soon as his horn blew, groups of workers would steal away to the woods. There the grownups listened to Cudjoe read the Bible and exchanged news which had come to them over the grapevine telegraph. High up in the trees above them,

sharp-eared youngsters kept watch, ready to hoot like owls if there was a sign of patrollers.

Harriet learned the paths through the underbrush and how to imitate the calls of the birds. Each Sunday she and Daddy Ben went for a walk, exploring the woods that Ben had known since he was a small boy. He showed her his old hiding places, the caves and hollow trees and sheltered spots deep in the forest. When she grew hungry, he taught her which berries and leaves were good to eat and which would make her sick, where the best nuts grew in autumn and the clearest, coldest springs bubbled over the ground.

On the way home, he made Harriet take the lead. If she got twisted in her direction, he patiently pointed out the green moss on the oaks and pines which could be her guide.

"Moss on the north side of the trees by day and the North Star at night. You can always go by them," Ben told his daughter.

This was how Harriet, who did not have a last name, received her schooling on the Eastern Shore of Maryland thirty years before the Civil War. When her education was complete, she could neither read nor write nor add. To her, geography meant two points of the compass: South and North. History went back only a hundred years, starting with the

day her grandmother was kidnaped from a village on the African plains. Science was a knowledge of the sky and the forest, the North Star and the woodland paths to which it pointed.

But Harriet's school had taught her one important lesson until she knew it with her body, with her mind, and with her heart:

"Let my people go!"

The Train Whistle Blows

AT FIFTEEN, Harriet was a woman. She was not beautiful. Her hair was short and crinkly, her mouth large, her heavy-lidded eyes the blackest black. She was only five feet tall, and her broad, hard-muscled body was clothed in an ill-fitting castoff dress from the Big House, or in a coarse cotton shift. A red and yellow bandanna, wrapped tightly around her head to protect it from the glaring Maryland sun, was her only adornment.

Despite her plain appearance, there was a magnetic quality about Harriet. When she ran barefoot across the fields, with her head erect and her firm muscles rippling under her dark, lustrous skin, men and women stopped to admire her grace and strength.

"She's strong as any man," her brothers boasted. "She can beat the lot of you," Daddy Ben declared.

Tales of Harriet's strength spread across the plantation from the slave quarters to the Big House. When visitors arrived, Master brought them to the fields to see the sights. Leaning on their gold-headed canes and puffing their cigars of fine Maryland tobacco, the gentlemen marveled at the young girl who could lift huge hogsheads and pull a loaded wagon like an ox.

Conscious of their stares, Harriet's eyelids drooped over her shining eyes and her lower lip protruded, as it had done when she was a child. "They look at me as if I was an animal," she thought, and she deliberately turned her back on the gawking men.

Although she was a valuable field hand, performing the tasks of an able-bodied man, her sullen expression and rocklike chin made Master uncomfortable. There was a rebellious spirit here which had to be watched and curbed. When the price of tobacco took a sudden disastrous drop, and he found himself with more slaves than he could profitably work, Harriet was one of the first to be hired out to more prosperous neighboring farmers.

For a hundred dollars a year, paid in gold to Master on New Year's Day, she guided a plow beside the blue waters of the Bay or clucked to a team of oxen along the muddy Choptank River. Up and down

the Eastern Shore, never more than a few miles from her parents' home, she corded wood in the oak forests in winter and planted and weeded under the summer sun.

It was while working in Bucktown for a farmer named Barrett that Harriet met Jim. Everyone knew Barrett's Jim. Twice that year he had run away, only to be captured and brought back in chains. Looking at him, tall, strong, brave enough to stand the hardest whipping without crying out, everyone knew that he would run away again.

Harriet liked to listen to Jim's stories of his travels. Last spring he had gotten as far as Baltimore. He had seen the new steam engines with locomotives like giant teakettles. Puffing clouds of black smoke, they pulled wooden coaches all the way to Washington.

"Sixty passengers at one time," Jim marveled. "But before a black man can ride, he has to show papers saying he's free."

He told her also of another railroad. " 'Tain't as comfortable as the Baltimore and Ohio," he grinned. "Everyone furnish his own car and his own steam to make it go. But the Underground Railroad's got some mighty fine conductors."

Slaves had been escaping from the South for as long as there was slavery. They traveled through swamps and along riverbanks, hiding in haystacks by

day and plodding along back roads in the dark of night, their only friend the North Star. Now there was a growing community of people, North and South, who believed that slavery should be abolished. At the risk of lives and livelihoods, they were banding together to hide the footsore men and feed the hungry girls.

On the banks of the Ohio River, just a few years earlier, a slave disappeared while in sight of his pursuing master. Puzzled and angry, his owner proclaimed, "He must have gone on an underground road." The name stuck, and when the first steam-drawn cars ran on rails between Baltimore and Washington, the slave routes to freedom were called the "Underground Railroad."

Jim had heard of homes even in Maryland and Delaware where a knock on the door, day or night, would bring a hearty meal and a good bed and a safe hiding place. The "stations" on the Underground Railroad were houses and barns; the "conductors," free Negroes, kindly Quakers, ministers, working-men. A farm wagon or peddler's cart served as passenger car, a horse as locomotive.

"The only ticket you need is a black skin." Jim lowered his voice to a whisper.

"White men help us?" Harriet asked, as she had asked Old Cudjoe.

"White men and black." Jim nodded. And he

talked about Thomas Garrett, the Wilmington Quaker who sold shoes to slaveholders while he hid their fleeing property in a secret room above his store. Of William Still, a free Negro who headed the Anti-Slavery Society office in the free city of Philadelphia. Of these and a dozen others in New York and Boston and Baltimore and Buffalo.

Jim and Harriet worked side by side all summer long, with the sun beating down on their backs and bare arms. When the leaves on the trees turned red and gold and a cool breeze came in from the Bay, Jim was restless. Evenings, cleaning the wheat and husking corn in the barn, he sang:

> That Gospel Train is comin';
> I hear it 'round the curve,
> She's loosened all her steam and brakes
> And straining every nerve.
>
> The fare is cheap and all can go,
> The rich and poor is there;
> No second class aboard this train,
> No difference in the fare.
>
> Get on board, little chillun
> Get on board, little chillun
> Get on board, little chillun,
> There's room for many a more.

As Harriet joined in the chorus, she knew what train Jim was thinking about. He'd soon be on his way.

On one of these cool September nights, when fingers ached from stripping a mountain of corn ears, Jim abruptly announced that he was out of tobacco.

"Going to walk to the crossroads store and get some." His tone was casual, but he looked for a long moment at Harriet before he slid the barn door closed behind him.

The slaves crouched around the long plank table began to work at a feverish pace. Through the hayloft door they could see the new moon, a thin sliver in a starry sky. The night was dark, the North Star shining. If only the overseer, at home eating supper, would linger over an extra glass of wine. If only he would not notice Jim's absence when he returned. Harriet's fingers fumbled as she reached for another ear of corn. Her heart was pounding.

Minutes passed before the barn door squeaked open. The overseer glanced around the room, counting noses. "Where's Jim?" he growled.

No one answered. In the silence, Harriet was sure that he could hear the noise her heart was making. She bent her head to hide the hope that was in her eyes.

"I thought I saw a fellow going down the road. If that rascal's run off again — " He didn't stay to finish the sentence. Turning on his heel, he ran in the direction Jim had taken.

Harriet's ear of corn bounced across the table and

her stool crashed to the floor. While the overseer followed the road, she cut across the fields. Breathing hard, she reached the store before him. Jim was there, whispering to the man behind the counter. Before she had a chance to warn him of the danger, the overseer strode in.

"You there, Jim," he ordered. "Get back to the barn this instant. I'll whip you for this."

Cautiously, Jim circled away from the outstretched hands. As the overseer neared the counter, he sidestepped toward the door. Harriet, flattened against the wall and, scarcely daring to breathe, touched his shoulder as he passed.

"Grab him, Harriet," the overseer bellowed. "Hold him for me while I tie him up."

In a flash, Harriet had moved to the doorway. Calmly, she stretched out her arms to block the overseer's pursuit. Outside, Jim was running for the sheltering woods.

Beside himself with rage, the overseer picked up a two-pound weight from the storekeeper's scales. He threw it after the retreating figure, but Jim was far out of range. The weight struck Harriet in the forehead. She fell to the ground with a moan.

An hour later, Mr. Barrett carried her into her parents' cabin and threw her on Old Rit's patchwork quilt. "She's dying," he said over his shoulder as he left the tiny cluttered room.

Not Worth a Sixpence

Dying, Harriet seemed to be. Unconscious for days, racked by fever and pain, she lay on her pallet of straw and rags. Tearfully Old Rit nursed her, putting moist cloths on her aching forehead. Tenderly Daddy Ben watched over her, fetching cool spring water and pleading with her to eat. It was weeks before Harriet knew what had happened, months before someone whispered that Jim had made his way across the line to become a free man.

When she first opened her eyes and could turn herself over in bed, her face was dull and her voice soft and toneless. She felt unable to move, unable to speak, unable to think. Everything in her mind was cloudy, and she slept long hours at a stretch, waking

only to go back to sleep again. It was as if she were suspended halfway between life and death.

While she slept, she had strange vivid dreams which went back over her whole life and the life of her people. Once she saw the bloodstained deck of a sailing vessel like the ones on which slaves were carried from Africa. Black men were standing on the deck, unfettered, with white men lying wounded and dead at their feet.

Then Jim's stories of the Underground Railroad seemed to be happening to her. She dreamed of flying over fields and mountains, looking down on cities like a bird. At last she would reach a high fence or a wide river, and her strength would leave her. Just as she was sinking down, ladies dressed in white came to her rescue.

She told some of these dreams to Daddy Ben. "I seemed to see a line, and on the other side of the line were green fields and lovely flowers and beautiful white ladies who stretched out their arms to me over the line. But I couldn't reach them. I always fell before I got to the line."

Ben's chin set hard. "One of these days, child, you're going to find that line. Rest now to get your strength, so you can march right over it on your own two feet."

All through the fall and winter, Harriet stayed in

her parents' cabin. On Christmas Day, thin and list-
less, she got up for the first time. Soon she was able
to spend a few hours a day out of bed, helping with
the household chores. The scar on her forehead healed
clean, but the iron weight had fractured her skull, leaving a permanent dent and a pressure on her brain
which caused sudden sleeping spells. These spells were
to be with her for the rest of her life.

The first time Old Rit found Harriet leaning on the
broom handle, fast asleep while sweeping the floor,
she screamed until Ben came running to the cabin.

"She'll never be right," Rit cried, "and it's all because she wouldn't listen to me. When the white folks
talk to her, she just close her eyes and puff out her
mouth, full of hate. The Bible says 'love, love.'"

"Bible says 'hate' too," Ben mildly observed. He
leaned over to pat Harriet's thin hand, and her eyes
blinked open. Without a word, she started to sweep
again.

She fell asleep on her way to the spring for water,
propped against the fence with the bucket hanging
heavy in her hand. She slept suddenly, briefly, while
cooking or sewing or spreading the wash on the
bushes to dry. The drowsiness overtook her even
when she was talking. For a few minutes her eyes
would close and her chin droop to her chest. Then
she would shake her head and continue the conver-
sation as if there had been no interruption.

Soon family and friends became used to these spells and ceased to marvel at them. If they noticed them at all, it was only to say, "Look at Hat. Gone off again."

Slowly Harriet regained her strength. With the first warm days of spring, she went back to work in the fields. Old Rit sighed as she watched her sing the chorus of a forbidden song as soon as the overseer's back was turned.

"Harriet's her old self again," she complained to William Henry. "Born for trouble."

But Harriet was not her old self again. The blow on her head had changed her life, and it could never be the same. During the long painful months in the cabin, she had thought things out carefully until one clear fact emerged. Singlehanded, she had fought against slavery and had survived. She was no longer only a piece of property, like the horses and cows who dumbly did Master's bidding. While still a slave in form, she was in spirit a human being and a free woman.

The blow on her head had also changed her in Master's eyes. When she was brought home, more dead than alive, he vowed to sell her if she recovered. Her act of defiance, resulting in the loss of a valuable slave, could not go unpunished. Day after day, he led prospective buyers to her cabin. The well-dressed

planters pulled back Harriet's covers to pinch her and poke her and measure her girth as they might a horse. But noting her glazed eyes and wasted flesh and the deep dent in her forehead, they one by one shook their heads.

Even when she was on her feet again and her thin body had begun to fill out, no one was willing to buy her. Once she fell asleep in front of two traders, awakening to hear their disgusted voices.

"She'll never give an honest day's work."

"Not worth sixpence."

After that, whenever Master brought a buyer to inspect her, Harriet pretended to sleep. Slowly her eyes closed and her face became an expressionless mask. Not until they had pronounced her hopeless and taken their leave did she lift her sagging head. Then one eye would open, and when she winked at Benjie, the two would laugh aloud.

So convincing was her pose that before the year was out Master believed that he had a useless piece of merchandise on his hands. Other girls her age were forced to marry so that they would bear strong slave children to work for the land. But Harriet was not considered suitable even for "breeding."

"That half-wit!" Miss Sarah sniffed. "Marry her off, and we'll soon have a parcel of young idiots staring stupidly at us, just like their mother."

"Afraid you're right, my dear," Master agreed. "The only thing to do with Harriet is to let her hire her own time. That way we're sure of some return, and when she has spells we won't have her on our hands."

Hiring one's own time was usually a reward for faithful service. To Harriet it meant that she could take any job she could find, so long as she paid her owner a sum of money for the privilege of working. Master demanded one dollar each week, rain or shine, sick or well. Whatever money she earned beyond that was her own. It would be a hard life, but there was hope in it.

"Here's your chance, girl," Daddy Ben advised. "It don't take much to fill your stomach and cover your back. You save your money, and some day you can buy yourself from Master."

Harriet was not sure that Ben was right. She dreamed of a faster road to freedom, the starlit path which Jim had followed. But Jim's path was lonely, and there was danger there. Ben's would keep her close to her family and the rich green country-side which she loved. When Ben offered to speak to Mr. Stewart about her, she nodded agreement.

John Stewart, who rented Ben from Master by the year, was a lumberman and builder. He supplied oak masts for sailing vessels and fine-grained pine to

panel the plantation parlors. Ben was his timber in-
spector, boss of a gang of men in the woods, and he
was glad to find work for Ben's daughter.

At first Harriet scrubbed floors and scraped pots in
the Stewart household. Later she was assigned to the
fields and forest. Despite the sleeping spells which
might overtake her when she was lifting a barrel or
guiding a plow, she worked steadily. When the sun
went down on Saturday night, she trudged along
dusty back roads to pay her dollar to Master and
visit over Sunday with her mother and father.

Each week Harriet put aside a few pennies from
her meager earnings. They rattled around in the hol-
lowed-out gourd in which she kept them until they
added up to dollars. One dollar, two dollars, three
dollars. By Christmastime, there were ten dollars in
the gourd; by spring, twenty.

One Saturday night, when the coins had filled the
gourd to overflowing, Harriet dared to ask Master
if she could buy herself from him.

"How much you sell me for?" Her voice was
hoarse, and her eyes fixed firmly on his shiny leather
boots.

Master threw back his head and laughed. That this
half-mad creature could ever hope to earn enough
money to buy her freedom was uproariously funny.
"Five hundred dollars," he announced. "When you

bring me five hundred good United States dollars, you'll get your free papers." He laughed again.

Harriet's heart sank, but the expression on her face never changed. Once outside, she stopped to calculate. She now had twenty-two dollars hidden in her parents' cabin. "Rate I'm going it'll take a lifetime to get five hundred," she figured.

With the sound of Master's laughter in her ears, she worked harder than ever. From dawn to dark, six days a week, she weeded and hoed in John Stewart's fields. Nights she took in washing from a widower down the road and baked pies to sell in Bucktown. Winters she trapped muskrats on the salt marshes. Summers she caught crabs in the blue inlets of the Bay. When there was a cotillion on Saturday night or a tea party on Sunday, she hired herself out as an extra hand in the kitchen. There was always firewood to be chopped and rails to split, if she could lift her aching arms to swing an ax.

She filled a second gourd and a third, but it was not enough. When she could count out forty dollars, she begged for an afternoon off and a pass to Cambridge. By the light of the moon she returned, driving a pair of steers which she had purchased with her savings. That night her rich voice rang out in the song of Moses, without a thought for the patroller who might be hidden around a bend in the road.

With Ben speaking up for her, Mr. Stewart permitted Harriet to work a piece of his land. It was a cut-over wood lot, covered with stumps and dried weed stalks, and it sloped sharply down to the yellow waters of the Choptank. Each night at dusk, each morning before the overseer's horn called her to work, Harriet was out with her steers. Together they pulled the stumps and plowed up the weeds and graded the soil until it could be planted. In the fall, Harriet borrowed a wagon and hauled her first crops to the Cambridge market.

Walking past the trim brick houses and tree-shaded lawns in Cambridge with her ticking bag stuffed with money, Harriet was suddenly reluctant to go home. She was tired, bone-tired, and she dreaded starting her endless round of work again. Across the street on the courthouse steps, a tall young man smiled at her. She hesitated for only a moment. Then she crossed the road to sit down beside him.

John Tubman was much like Jim in appearance, but in one important way he was different. John was a free man. With his head held high, he could collect his wages each Saturday and spend them as he chose. True, he was prevented by Maryland law from owning a dog or carrying a gun or attending a church without a white minister. His life was bound

by a hundred rules, written and unwritten, just as Harriet's was. But he was free. He owned himself and need call no man "Master."

Carefree and gay, John whistled and joked. He and Harriet laughed together like little children. She began to sing again, not the forbidden freedom songs, but the lullabies and nonsense verses she had learned long ago from Old Rit. This was a different kind of happiness than Harriet had ever felt before. Soon she knew that she loved John Tubman with all her heart. In the spring of the year, when the furry buds on the magnolias opened and the mockingbirds sang their sweetest, they were married.

John moved into Harriet's cabin in the Stewart slave quarters, and she struggled to make it into a home for him. While he sang to her by the light of the fire at night, she pieced together scraps of cloth until she had finished a patchwork quilt which was as warm and beautiful as Old Rit's.

In slave territory, there was little opportunity for a free Negro to find work. So long as he had a roof over his head and food to eat, John was not one to worry. He hunted and fished, and he laughed and sang, and for a time that was enough.

Slowly Harriet found her savings going. There was food to be bought for John, clothing for John, and tobacco. If she scolded him for his extravagance or

begged him to look for work, he'd throw back his head and laugh, teasing her until she joined in with him.

But love could not long provide an escape from slavery for Harriet Tubman. The nights of happiness soon alternated with nights of bitter quarrels. John saw little wrong with their way of life, and he mocked at his wife's burning desire to be free.

"There have always been masters and slaves," he would tell her. "You can't change things."

For her part, she scolded and nagged until he fled to the crossroads store to escape her angry voice. Alone in the cabin then, she pulled the quilt around her shoulders and studied the stars through the cracks in the roof. Her gourds were almost empty, but the North Star was still there.

It was on a blistering Sunday in the summer of 1849 that the big blow fell. Master was dead. Slumped in his chair in the parlor of the Big House, he had drawn his last breath before the doctor could be called. As the news spread to the quarters, there was terror in every heart.

"What will Miss Sarah do?" Old Rit cried. "She'll sell us to the cotton planters, sure as you're born. We'll never see each other for the rest of our mortal lives."

Nothing could stop the old woman's tears. Leaving her with Ben, Harriet raced across the fields to

talk to her husband. John was asleep when she reached the cabin.

She shook him vigorously. "Master's dead. They say we'll all be sold."

John blinked as he swung his long legs to the floor. "Nonsense," he yawned. "You're always imagining trouble. Master's dead? You'll get a new master."

Harriet lost all patience. "Mistress always hated me. And Benjie and William Henry too. She's sure to get rid of us." She lowered her voice, pronouncing each word separately and distinctly. "I'm — going — to — run — away."

Now it was John's turn to be angry. "Don't be a fool, woman. You can't make it. Those dogs will track you down 'fore you're out of the county. Then it'll go worse for you. You're not going." He grabbed her wrist.

Shaking herself free, Harriet stood up. Without another word, she left the cabin. She knew what she had to do.

Bound for the Promised Land

Long ago Jim had told Harriet about the white people called Quakers, the plain folk whose gray or black dress and gentle speech hid a burning hatred of slavery. "Quakers almost as good as colored," he'd chuckled. "They call themselves Friends, and you can trust them every time."

When she was selling pies from door to door in Bucktown, Harriet noticed a tiny blond woman whose bonnet and dress marked her as one of the "good" white people. Silently she had followed her home. Standing half hidden behind a tree, she had studied her neat brick cottage and the white picket fence which enclosed a garden of hollyhocks and delphiniums and a yard of squawking chickens.

Now, after her quarrel with John, Harriet made for the Stewart kitchen. Borrowing a market basket, she set off down the road. Across the creek, past a cornfield, and then the brick house was in sight. Despite her anger and her fear, her movements were deliberate. She had thought about this for a long time.

"Watch your step now," she whispered as she unhooked the gate. "Got to act just right."

At the door of the house she hesitated, then boldly lifted the brass knocker. The latch clicked and the door swung back. The tiny lady in gray smiled questioningly at her.

"Please, mistress. I saw your hens and I thought maybe you'd sell me some eggs. I have money to pay." Harriet pointed to her basket.

"I'm afraid I couldn't sell thee eggs on First Day. But thee looks hot. Won't thee come in and drink some lemonade?"

Harriet nodded. The interview was proceeding as she had hoped it would. She followed her hostess to the parlor, trying not to look frightened. This was her first experience as a guest in a white household. "Careful, careful!" she warned herself.

The lemonade was cool and sweet, and Harriet's voice was steady when she asked, "Do you know Master Garrett up in Wilmington? I hear he's a Quaker, just like yourself."

"I don't know a *Master* Garrett." The white woman smiled as she emphasized the word. "Thomas Garrett lets no man or woman call him 'Master.'"

Harriet looked up with an answering smile, but she hesitated to go on. This was so easy that it might be a trap.

Pretending not to notice her visitor's uncertainty, the Quaker continued, "I have visited Thomas Garrett many times, breaking my journey with the Hunn family. Does thee know of Ezekiel Hunn in Camden, or John Hunn in Middletown?"

Breathless, Harriet shook her head.

"Both good men. Thee would like them. Were I traveling, I would follow the Choptank River north to its source, just at the border between Maryland and Delaware. The road there runs straight to Camden. North by east, it's fifteen miles to Ezekiel's. A clapboard house with green shutters and a red brick chimney. Any — " She hesitated to find the right word. "Any workingman can point it out. The railroad goes through Camden now, thee knows."

Harriet's eyes sparkled, and her lips curved in their broadest smile. "Sure would like to meet *Mister* Hunn and *Mister* Garrett. Everyone talking about that new railroad. I've been wanting to try it for a long, long time."

The Quaker poured more lemonade into Harriet's

glass. "In case thee should be going, I wonder if thee'd mind carrying a message for Ezekiel?"

While Harriet finished her drink, her hostess wrote a few words on a piece of paper. Gravely, Harriet stowed the note in her market basket and made ready to depart.

"Let me give thee a few eggs, so that thy trip won't have been wasted." The Quaker's blue eyes twinkled.

"This trip's not wasted," Harriet grinned back. "But in case I meet someone on the road, be a good idea to have the eggs."

At the door, the two women reached out at the same moment to shake hands. "Godspeed," the Quaker whispered, and Harriet, too moved to speak, smiled her thanks.

Trudging down the road, Harriet thought fleetingly of John. Should she share with him the paper in her basket and its promise for the future? "No." She shook her head. "This is for my brothers and me. John can't be trusted."

Instead of turning off at the Stewart plantation, she headed for her parents' cabin. Benjamin and William Henry and her older brother, Robert, were still excitedly discussing Master's death and the change it could mean in their lives. Fearful that Old Rit might unwittingly give away her secret, Harriet kept silent until she could speak to her brothers alone.

Outside, under the oak tree where Old Cudjoe had read the story of Moses, she told them of her plans. "Next Saturday night we start," she concluded. "That way we'll have all day Sunday before they notice we're missing. By the time that alarm goes out on Monday — " She left the sentence unfinished.

Each brother entered his protest. The hound dogs, the patrollers, the unknown paths through woods and swamps, the armed posses, and the cold loneliness of the North.

"Let's wait," Robert urged. "Let's see what Mistress does."

"Wait!" Even in a whisper, Harriet's tone could be fierce. "I'm not waiting no longer. I reasoned this out in my mind. There are two things I have a right to, liberty or death. If I can't have one, I'll have the other. I'll fight for my liberty as long as my strength lasts, and when the time comes for me to go, the Lord will let them take me."

The silence was heavy. Then William Henry nodded. "I'll go, Hat."

"I'll go." "I'll go," the other two agreed.

"Not a word to Daddy or Ma," Harriet cautioned. "Things'll be bad enough for them when we turn up missing. Mistress'll be shaking them, threatening them with her whip. But what they don't know, they can't tell. After a while, she'll have to let them be."

The next days dragged. All the time that Harriet was hoeing in the fields and cooking and scrubbing in the cabin, there was an excitement bubbling up inside her. Her mind raced furiously, planning routes and listing supplies for the trip. Toward John she turned a stolid face, lest he guess her plans. Although the two barely spoke in their last week together, it seemed to Harriet as if he were watching her every move.

On Saturday night it was raining hard when Harriet met her brothers in the woods. Clouds blotted out the moon and the star which was to guide them. For a mile or two they trudged along the paths they had followed as children. As the way became unfamiliar, they stumbled and twisted and turned in the blackness.

"It's no use, Hat." Robert shook his head. "We'll never make it."

"We could be going around in circles all night here, for all we know," Benjie glumly insisted.

"Can't make no time in this weather," William Henry agreed. "If we go back now, we'll live to try another time. Don't feel bad, Harriet." He patted his sister's hand.

In vain, Harriet argued and pleaded. The woods which they all knew so well had suddenly become peopled with unsuspected terrors and unknown fears.

Each time a twig snapped or a frog croaked, their hearts beat wildly. Anything could happen in the darkness which enveloped them. Drenched to the skin, they walked back in silence.

Heavy-hearted, Harriet proceeded to the Stewart plantation. John was snoring softly, but she could not sleep. Scene after scene flashed across her mind. Mistress running after her with a whip. The slave auction block in Cambridge. Her two sisters marching down the road, their wrists and ankles bound by heavy ropes. By morning, with the rain still pouring down, she had made her decision. "I'm going alone."

All day Sunday it rained, but Monday dawned clear and warm. Harriet went to the fields as usual. As she raised her hoe to bring it down heavily on a clump of weeds, she felt a tug at her dress. A small boy was standing next to her, his round eyes begging her to notice him. Recognizing him as Old Cudjoe's grandson, Harriet led him to the water bucket at the end of the row. While she sipped water from the broken gourd which served as dipper, he delivered his message.

"Grandpa says they going to sell you — you and your brothers. He thinks tonight the men come for you."

Patting the child's head, she whispered her thanks. When she had watched him scramble safely over the

fence, she squared her shoulders. "Tonight. I'm going for sure." It was a promise.

At the first sound of the overseer's horn, Harriet stowed her hoe in the shed and made for her cabin. Fortunately John was not at home. Into her ticking bag, to be tied around her waist, went all the things she would need: her week's food ration, the last remaining coins, and the sharp bowie knife which John used when he went hunting. Kicking off her tattered shoes, she thrust her feet into his new brogans.

"Won't he be mad now!" she grinned.

As she stood at the door for a final look around, her eyes fell on the patchwork quilt. Quickly stripping it from the bed, she folded it under her arm. The moon was shining when she tiptoed through the gate of the Quaker lady's yard. Silently she laid the quilt on the doorstep, feeling its warmth for the last time. This was thank you and farewell.

Now she was ready to leave, except for one thing. She must notify someone of her departure, or her parents would believe that she had been seized by the traders. It was not safe to visit their cabin, where her ticking bag and shiny shoes would surely give her away. Her sister, Mary Ann, still worked in the kitchen of the Big House. Perhaps she could talk with her without arousing suspicion.

The Big House kitchen was bustling with activity

when Harriet pushed back the screen door. Catching Mary Ann's eye, she beckoned her outside. Before they had a chance to exchange a word, Miss Sarah's brother rode by, turning in his saddle to glare at the two women. Frightened, Mary Ann ran back to her post. As the door slammed behind her, Harriet began to sing. Mary Ann caught the first words:

> When that old chariot comes,
> I'm going to leave you,
> I'm bound for the promised land.
> Friends, I'm going to leave you.

Past the slave quarters, with her ticking bag jogging at her waist, Harriet raised her voice so that all might hear:

> I'm sorry, friends, to leave you,
> Farewell! oh, farewell!
> But I'll meet you in the morning,
> Farewell! oh, farewell!

> I'll meet you in the morning
> When you reach the promised land;
> On the other side of the Jordan,
> For I'm bound for the promised land.

There were men and women and children in the cheerless cabins who never forgot the song they heard that night.

Following the Star

FOLLOW the Choptank to its source, the Quaker lady had said. Where the river flowed into the Bay it formed a busy harbor, lined with wharves and fishermen's huts and sailing vessels loading up for Baltimore. To keep away from this traffic, Harriet must walk cross-country through the woods and across the marshes, until the river narrowed to a muddy stream. Then only would it be safe to follow the Choptank.

With her eyes on the steady North Star, Harriet made her way through the woods. She had traveled the route many times in her mind, and she strode along confidently. When low-hanging branches tangled her hair and briars tore her legs, she scarcely noticed. Her heart was full of joy and her lips were

bursting with song. But she schooled herself to tramp in silence, conscious that every rock and bush might conceal an enemy in its shadow.

For hours she walked rapidly, covering the ground she had explored those long-ago Sundays with Daddy Ben. Friendly owls hooted from the trees, and in the distance she could hear the laughing call of the loon. As she reached unfamiliar territory, her pace slackened and she picked her way carefully through dense forest and over open swampy land. There were no paths, and in some places the vines of wild grape and bittersweet looped around the trees so densely that she could not break her way through.

When the moon was low in the sky and the stars fading, Harriet stopped to rest. She had traveled, she figured, most of the thirty miles she would have to go before she reached the Choptank. Too tired to go further, she sipped some water from a creek and stretched out on the mossy ground.

From the reeds, the bullfrogs honked. With the first slanting rays of the morning sun, the birds sang. Harriet heard none of them. For the first time in many months, she slept soundly.

When the midday sun found its way through the leaves to shine on her face, she jumped up, frightened. She was too near home to lie here in broad daylight. "They'll have the alarm out for me sure. Dogs'll find me if I don't get moving," she scolded herself.

Recklessly she plunged into the thicket. There was a noise in the underbrush and she broke into a run, only to find that she had circled back to the place where she had slept. For a moment she was panic-stricken. Without the North Star, how would she ever find the river?

Then she forced herself to be calm. The noise in the underbrush had been a rabbit, its twinkling tail a promise of food if she should need it. Daddy Ben had taught her how to travel in the daytime. Studying the base of the trees, she saw that on one side the moss grew thick and green. That way lay North.

A few minutes of steady walking, and Harriet could see in the distance a break in the deep woods. There the ground sloped sharply and the sun shone on the muddy waters of a narrow river. She had reached the Choptank.

Remembering the floppy-eared dogs sniffing at her trail many miles behind, she stooped to untie her shoes. Into the ticking bag they went, as she slid down the bank into the swirling water. For miles she waded through the river, ankle-deep, waist-high, until she had to hang her bag around her neck. She was thoroughly soaked, but the day was warm and she didn't care.

"For I'm bound for the promised land." Silently her lips formed the words of the song.

All afternoon she trudged upstream. The river

grew shallow, until it was nothing but a trickle of water bubbling over the rocks. As the sun set, Harriet
climbed up the muddy bank. Huddled in the hollow
of a dead oak tree, she tried to keep her teeth from
chattering while she ate some waterlogged bread and
soggy pork. It was far too early and too near home to
think of making a fire.

"Dogs'll have a hard time tracking me through
that water," she figured. "Now I got to say good-bye,
old Choptank, and head for Camden. North by east,
it's fifteen miles," she repeated the Quaker's directions.

In those fifteen miles she must leave the shadowy
woods for the open fields. In every house, at every
crossroads, there would be strangers watching out for
a fleeing black-skinned woman. Here the limbs of
the trees had sheltered her; there the arms of men
would be turned against her. Shivering in her damp
clothing, she laced up her shoes.

The sky was a deep blue, and the North Star shone
faintly when Harriet emerged from the woods.
Ahead of her a dusty highway stretched toward
Camden. Cautiously she tramped along, screening
herself from view behind the shrubs which edged the
road. The night was still, and for a long time the only
sounds came from her own footsteps. Then in the distance she heard the clatter of horses' hoofs.

She threw herself into a ditch, waiting for the riders to pass. Only a few yards ahead of her they dismounted and tied up their horses. With dismay, Harriet realized that they were building a fire. Inching along the rough ground on her stomach, she peered at them through the underbrush. There were four men, cooking and eating and passing a bottle of corn whiskey from mouth to mouth.

From their loud talk, Harriet learned that they were patrollers, riding the road in search of runaway slaves. When the firelight flickered on the silver butts of their pistols, she slipped her right hand into her bag. For an hour she watched, never loosening her grasp on John's bowie knife. Finally they took their leave, loudly damning the black folk who kept them from their beds on a night like this.

When they were out of earshot, Harriet stretched her cramped muscles and set off again. At each crossroad she stopped to check her direction with the stars. At each farm she circled fields and barn, lest a dog betray her with his bark. By midnight, when she passed a cluster of stores and a church, she was sure she had reached Camden. Now came the most dangerous part of her journey. She must find someone who would point out Ezekiel Hunn's house.

In the moonlight she could make out the outline of a ramshackle cabin, so poor that it must surely be-

long to a black man. She walked around it, studying out the best path to take if she should be wrong. Her knock on the door was answered by a frightened "Who's there?"

"It's me," Harriet whispered. "Can you tell me how to find Ezekiel Hunn?"

"Reckon I can," the voice inside mumbled. "Wait a minute."

It was a long minute, and Harriet swallowed her heart a dozen times as she waited. When the door creaked back, she could see that she was talking to a tall woman, dark of skin.

"You sure scared me, knocking on the door in the middle of the night," the stranger complained. "But I work for Mr. Hunn, so I ought to be used to it. His house is right over the hill. You can see the chimney from here when it's light."

Murmuring her thanks, Harriet followed the woman's pointing finger. A quarter of a mile along the road and she came to a clapboard house with a broad brick chimney. The house was dark, each window heavily shuttered.

"Day or night, they take us in," she thought. "Should I wake up the family?

"No." Her habit of mistrust asserted itself. "Better wait till morning and see what they look like first."

There were haystacks in the meadow behind the

barn and Harriet crawled into one, pulling the sweet-smelling grass around her. It was good to rest and feel warm. Her eyes closed and her head began to nod.

Suddenly she jerked herself awake. She couldn't sleep now. She must watch and wait until she was sure she was safe. Regretfully she left the hay to spend the rest of the night pacing back and forth in the shelter of the barn. She dared not sit down, lest sleep overtake her.

When the morning sun had dried the dew on the grass, the back door of the house swung open. A woman dressed in gray began to sweep the steps. After watching her for a few minutes, Harriet went up to the woman and silently handed her the Quaker lady's note.

The woman's response was a strange one. With scarcely more than a glance at the note, she thrust the broom at Harriet.

"Sweep the yard," she whispered, and disappeared inside the house.

Riding on the Railroad

MECHANICALLY Harriet swept. The broom swished back and forth across the brick paving, raising puffs of dust. But Harriet's eyes were fixed on the house, and the muscles in her legs were tight, ready to carry her away if danger threatened.

She had to wait only a few minutes before the front door opened and two men emerged. One wore the black suit and broad-brimmed hat of Quaker men; the other was more fashionably attired. He strode to the barn to saddle a fine chestnut mare. With no more than a glance at the ordinary-looking woman who was sweeping, he leaped on his horse and galloped down the road.

As soon as the horseman was out of sight, the Quaker walked toward Harriet. "Thee are most welcome here." He smiled as he took the broom from her hands. "That man" — nodding toward the road — "is a slave trader. He was desirous of purchasing some of my hay, and he stopped the night with us. It is safe now to come inside.

"I am Ezekiel Hunn," he added as he held the door open for his visitor.

"And I am Harriet Tubman." She could barely form the words with her lips. The kindly Quaker voice, the warmth of the kitchen, and the smell of baking bread were suddenly too much for her. She stumbled and would have fallen had not her host caught her and led her to a chair.

"Thee is hungry, child, and tired. Thee must have food and rest, and then we shall make plans. Eliza!" he called to his wife.

After setting out a hearty breakfast, Mrs. Hunn led Harriet upstairs and put her to bed. When Harriet awoke, it was with a cry of wonder. The walls of the room were covered with flowers. A pattern of pink rosebuds and green leaves ran from floor to ceiling. There was a window of glass, where starched white curtains rustled in the summer breeze. Most wonderful of all was the bed, a great four-poster, fully three feet from the polished floor. Harriet stretched out

her arms and legs to feel its softness. Then she gently bounced up and down.

"Like resting on a cloud," she marveled.

All that day Harriet remained hidden indoors. After dark, Ezekiel Hunn hitched a team of horses to his wagon and drove her to the outskirts of Smyrna.

"I must turn back here to be home by dawn," he explained. "As thee knows, men are watching me too. If thee follows the road from here, thee can reach Middletown before daylight. My brother John will be looking for thee."

After describing John Hunn's house, he clucked to his team and headed homeward. Boldly, Harriet strode down the road, scorning to hide in the bushes as she had done the night before. The songs bubbling inside her spilled over. With her hand always on the handle of the knife in her ticking bag, she softly sang:

> When Israel was in Egypt's land,
> Let my people go.
> Oppressed so hard they could not stand,
> Let my people go.
>
> Go down, Moses,
> Way down in Egypt's land.
> Tell ole Pharaoh,
> Let my people go.

"It's coming true," she whispered. "I'm going to be free. Tomorrow, the next day, I'm going to be free!"

The night air was hot and heavy, and the only sign of life along the highway was an occasional barking dog. Toward dawn a rumble of thunder broke the silence. Sheets of rain turned the dusty road to mud, but Harriet slogged on, grateful for the cooling water on her cheeks. Then the rain stopped and the North Star faded in the morning sky. Dead ahead, in a little valley at the foot of a hill, lay the house that Ezekiel Hunn had described.

The Hunns of Middletown were as kind as the Hunns of Camden. Harriet breakfasted and slept, and by the time she arose a message had gone to Thomas Garrett, telling him when to expect her. Wilmington, across the river from New Jersey and only eight miles from the Pennsylvania border, was as closely guarded as a medieval fortress. All bridges and roads leading to and from the city were patrolled, and Harriet would need an escort to guide her to Garrett's house.

"Unfortunately, I cannot take thee." John Hunn frowned. "Last year Friend Garrett and I were hauled to the court at New Castle and convicted of the dreadful crime of sheltering a runaway mother and her six children. My carriage in front of Thomas' house now would signal an army of constables to his door. Thee must walk alone, following the road, until thee comes to the first Wilmington bridge. On a hill

overlooking the river, thee will see a graveyard. Hide among the headstones there, until a conductor comes for thee. He will say, 'I bring you a ticket for the railroad.'"

The first lap of the twenty-three-mile journey to Wilmington was made in John Hunn's carriage. "This is a great country for slave catchers," he cautioned when he left. "There's a reward out for thee, so look sharp." With a friendly handclasp, he headed for home.

On this, Harriet's fourth night on the road, she was too weary to sing. Thick clouds hid the friendly North Star, and she plodded along, past fields and barns, past creeks and towns, wishing for an end to her journey. After leaving New Castle, one of her sleeping spells overtook her. She awakened to hear a horse's whinny.

There was a group of mounted men only a few feet away. Harriet dug her fingernails into the bark of the tree against which she was leaning. These were the dreaded slave catchers, on the prowl for runaways. Frozen to the tree trunk, she held her breath. Surely they could hear the insistent beat of her heart.

"Devil take the wench," a gruff voice swore. "She can't have gotten further than this. Edwards saw Hunn's carriage near Smyrna."

"Best give up for now," a companion counseled.

"Can't see our fingers in front of our faces. She's headed for Wilmington, sure. We'll pick her up there in the morning."

Grunting assent, the horsemen trotted slowly in the direction of Wilmington. But they might double back on their tracks at any time. The road was no longer safe.

Feeling her way with hands outstretched, Harriet stumbled across the adjacent fields. In the blackness of the night, she climbed fences, waded streams, and sloshed through bogs. Every few yards she forced herself to crawl back through the underbrush and find the highway, to make sure that she was still heading north.

The somber night became a murky day. Through the morning mist, Harriet could make out the outlines of a bridge. To the east of it, rocky ground sloped upward. She climbed until she could feel the smooth cold marble of a gravestone. Then she tumbled to the ground.

As she fought to keep awake, she felt a light tap on her shoulder. Her hand slid into her bag, hunting for John's knife. Before she could pull it out, a friendly voice whispered, "I bring you a ticket for the railroad."

Harriet's ticket was a suit of men's clothes and a rake. With her dress and hair concealed by overalls

and cap, she walked across the bridge beside her companion. To passers-by, the two were clearly Negro workingmen on their way to jobs in the city of Wilmington. On the street on which Thomas Garrett lived, her guide left her.

"Go to the back door and knock three times," he counseled. "They're waiting for you."

When the door opened, Harriet found her hand in the hearty clasp of Thomas Garrett, stationmaster of the Underground Railroad. After their greeting, Garrett hustled her up his stairs. On the second-floor landing a bookcase crammed with leather-bound volumes blocked their way. With a flourish, Garrett removed two of the books. Behind them a brass doorknob gleamed. As Harriet stared, the bookcase swung out, revealing a tiny windowless room.

"The waiting room of the railroad," Garrett smiled. "Only friends know of its existence. My shoe store is beneath, so thee must be quiet here."

For two days Harriet lived in Thomas Garrett's hidden room. "Thy mistress has put out handbills announcing thy escape," he explained, "and the slave catchers are all watching for thee. On First Day morning, when they are in church, thee will leave Wilmington in my carriage. Once thee is out of the city, thee can walk to the Pennsylvania border, and from there to Philadelphia. But even in the free

states, thee must be on guard. There are worthless wretches there who would not hesitate to kidnap thee for a reward."

On Sunday morning, six days after Harriet had left her Maryland home, Thomas Garrett took her arm and led her to his carriage. John's fine shoes, muddy and torn until her toes showed through the splitting seams, had been discarded. In their place she wore a new pair from Garrett's store. Her clothes were washed and mended, and a heavy black veil concealed her features. To all appearances, she was a lady out for a ride with her genial host.

Outside the city, Garrett stopped the horses. "The path here is well worn, and thee cannot miss it. An hour's good walking will bring thee to the highway. A wooden signpost there marks the line between Delaware and Pennsylvania. Step past that sign, and thee is free! Godspeed." He pressed a silver dollar into her hand.

Harriet's feet flew over the narrow path. In less than an hour she had followed its twists and turns until she could see the highway ahead. After peering out cautiously to make sure that she was alone, she stepped to the signpost at the crossing. With her head held high, she walked into the free state of Pennsylvania.

She stood there, wanting to sing, wanting to shout,

but no sounds came. A tear glistened on her cheek, and she wiped it away.

"I looked at my hands," she later told a friend, "to see if I was the same person now I was free. There was such a glory over everything. The sun came like gold through the trees and over the fields, and I felt like I was in heaven."

In a Strange Land

I~N HARRIET'S DREAMS~ there had been beautiful ladies with their arms outstretched to greet her as she crossed the line to freedom. Now, standing in the sunlight, breathing the free air, she was alone.

A carriage passed, crowded with a family in Sunday-best, but no one leaned from the window to talk to her. A young couple strolled by, hand in hand, but they scarcely glanced at her. When she spoke to a little girl who was swinging on a farmhouse gate, the child was frightened and ran crying into the house.

Squaring her shoulders, Harriet trudged along the highway. She was thirsty, but she hesitated to knock on a door to ask for water. She was tired, but she had no bed in which to rest.

"I'm a stranger in a strange land," she mused. "My home, after all, is down in the cabin quarter with the old folks and my brothers and sister.

"But I'm free." She was almost shouting now. "And they shall be free also. I will make a home for them in the North, and the Lord helping me, I will bring them all here."

It was dusk before she could see in the distance the outlines of Philadelphia's homes and stores. Sitting by the side of the road, she opened the supper that Mrs. Garrett had packed. When the moon was high in the sky, she slept on the damp ground. Awakened by the morning sun, she felt refreshed and steady of purpose. A half hour's walk brought her to the streets of the city, and she set about looking for work.

Philadelphia in 1849 was a bustling metropolis, its streets crowded with tradesmen and morning shoppers. No one had time to notice Harriet or to wonder where she had come from. Past the business district she walked, until she came to rows of houses with neat porches fronting on broad streets. In the rear of each home, a busy housewife was shaking a mop from the upstairs window or hanging out clothes on a crowded line.

Harriet knocked at three back doors before she found a woman who nodded and beckoned her in. For a week she washed walls and floors and beat out carpets in a tiny yard. The hours were almost as long

as on the plantation, but when Saturday night rolled around, the woman paid her two silver dollars. Clutching them in her hand, Harriet ran outside. By the light of the street lamp, she examined them.

"They're mine," she exulted, "and no master can take them from me. My hands are my own now and I can earn more dollars next week and next."

Next week Harriet earned her two dollars again. Then she sought out a new employer in another section of the city. Knocking on Philadelphia's back doors, she became laundress, scrubwoman, cook, seamstress. Changing jobs frequently was a part of her new-found freedom.

On Sundays, still a stranger in a strange land, she headed for the highway to spend happy hours tramping through the fields and the forest. When the northern winter brought icy winds and snowdrifts on the roads, she began to make her way around Philadelphia.

The houses were gay with tinsel and holly now, and the store windows crowded with dazzling Christmas gifts. Marveling at these, Harriet passed them by to spend her earnings in a dusty pawnshop. Her purchase at Christmas was a heavy silver pistol.

Many times that winter she walked to Mary Street, standing outside a public school in which Negro children were learning to read and write. From there she turned to Chestnut Street, to visit the old

brick building where American freedom had had its birth. Entering Independence Hall, her mind went back to Old Cudjoe's stories.

In the great chamber of the Hall stood the bell which had rung out for liberty. Running her hand over its polished surface, Harriet wished she could read the writing around its crown. In the noisy Sunday crowd she caught the eye of a dignified man who seemed to be watching her. Boldly she addressed him.

"Those words on the bell — what do they say?"

In ringing tones, so that all in the room turned their heads to listen, the gentleman read: " 'Proclaim liberty throughout all the land, to all the inhabitants thereof.'

"Good words," he added. "We must make them come true."

This was the kind of talk Harriet liked to hear. The dignified man introduced himself as William Still, secretary of the Pennsylvania Anti-Slavery Society. In a few minutes Harriet had made her first friend in Philadelphia.

Walking through the park, Still told Harriet of the long routes of the eastern branch of the Underground Railroad which converged in Philadelphia. All north-bound traffic in human cargo, by sea, by land, on foot, or in the coaches of the steam cars, passed

through the office of the Anti-Slavery Society. Black conductors in the mountains of Kentucky, white brakemen in the shadow of the Capitol dome in Washington, sea captains on the New Orleans run, all shipped their freight through him.

Daily his mail warned him to expect "five large packages and three small ones," "two bales of black wool," "four of God's poor." As secretary of the Society, Still kept a careful record of each "package" in his journal.

"Who held them in bondage, how they had been treated, what prompted them to escape, and whom that were near and dear to them they had left in chains," he explained. "Long after they're settled on farms in the Hudson Valley, or in the seacoast towns of New England, they keep in touch with me. Through the Underground Railroad they are often able to buy their wives and children, one by one, or to hire a conductor to lead their families to the North."

Still's stories were like a key unlocking a door. For months Harriet had said nothing beyond "Good day" or "Yes ma'am." Now the words poured out her hopes, her dreams, her loneliness in the North.

"I knew of a man," she told Still, "who was sent to the State Prison for twenty-five years. All these years he was always thinking of his home, and counting by

years, months, and days the time till he should be
free and see his family and friends once more. The
years roll on. The time of imprisonment is over. The
man is free. He leaves the prison gates. He makes his
way to his old home, but his old home is not there.
The house in which he had dwelt in his childhood
had been torn down, and a new one had been put up
in its place. His family were gone. Their very name
was forgotten. There was no one to take him by the
hand to welcome him back to life.

"So it is with me," Harriet said. "I've crossed the
line of which I have so long been dreaming. I'm free,
but there is no one to welcome me to the land of freedom. I must bring my people here and build a home
for them."

Still nodded sympathetically. Other fugitives he
had talked with felt this way. "There are men who
travel to the Eastern Shore," he suggested. "Perhaps
they can get in touch with your people."

"No!" Harriet's eyes flashed. "There are three mil-
lion of my people on the plantations in the South. I
must go down, like Moses into Egypt, to lead them
out."

She told Still of the dollars clinking against the pistol at the bottom of her ticking bag. "Soon as there's
enough money, I plan to start."

"But once you step over the line, you're a slave

again," he pointed out the dangers. "If they catch you, they'll sell you to the Deep South, sure as you're born."

"*If* they catch me."

"Don't even have to do that," Still argued. "The rewards for runaways say 'dead or alive.' With a black woman on the highway or hanging around the fields, the patrollers like as not will shoot first and ask questions afterward.

"Our conductors are all men," he continued. "White men whose safety has often depended on the color of their skin, or black men with papers at least to prove they're free-born."

"Nobody asked whether I was man or woman when they put an ax in my hand or tied me by the waist to a mule," Harriet interrupted. "I been doing man's work all my life. I'm not afraid."

Studying her erect head and bright eyes, Still believed her. She was not afraid. She would return to the land of bondage and set her people free. In his journal, soon to be filled with accounts of her adventures, he wrote, "She seems wholly devoid of personal fear. The idea of being captured by slave hunters or slaveholders seems never to enter her mind."

"Why Not Every Man?"

AFTER A SUMMER working as a cook at a resort hotel on the Jersey coast, after one year of freedom, Harriet Tubman entered Maryland again. Her sister, Mary Ann, William Still had learned, was to be sold at public auction from the courthouse in Cambridge. While the auctioneer was at lunch, Mary Ann's husband freed her from the slave pen and hid her in a nearby house. Late that night, with their two children, they sailed up the Bay to Baltimore in a rented fishing smack. There Harriet was waiting for them.

With three apprentices from the shipyards who also desired a change of scene, they traveled northward. Harriet led them through the woods and the sleeping towns to the homes of friends. They slept in

potato holes in the kitchen floor, in haylofts and corn cribs, and on the wooden seats of Quaker meeting-houses. In a week's time they were in Philadelphia.

Before the winter snow had melted from the roads, Harriet received an urgent message from James, her oldest brother. With the first thaw of spring, she set out to rescue him. James worked on a plantation in northern Maryland, not far from Wilmington. Accompanied by two friends, he stole away at night to meet his sister. Despite their caution, an overseer saw the men leave. Soon there was an alarm out for their capture.

Even in the woods, the fugitives were closely pursued. They could hear the noisy baying of the hounds when they came to a river. Its swirling waters looked deep, and there was no bridge or boat in sight.

"We must cross here." Harriet's decision was quickly made, but the men were panic-stricken and refused to move.

While they watched, Harriet plunged into the icy water. The river rose about her, to her knees, to her waist, to her armpits. It reached her chin, and they thought she was surely going under. Then, slowly, the water grew shallow again and Harriet was clambering up a slippery bank. Not until they could see her standing on the opposite shore, shivering in the raw March air, did James and his companions follow.

Pushing on through the night, the quartet waded a second stream before finding refuge in a freedman's cabin at the edge of the forest. By the time they reached the safety of Thomas Garrett's secret room, Harriet had given away her underclothing to repay the family who had sheltered them.

"When she called on me," Garrett wrote, "she was so hoarse she could hardly speak and she was also suffering with violent toothache."

Shaking with fever, Harriet led her party on until she could place them in the hands of William Still. She was ill for many months afterward.

Despite this illness, Harriet's first trips into slave territory were her least hazardous ones. Both had been arranged through correspondence with station-masters on the Underground Railroad, and on neither did she venture into the neighborhood of her old home. Now her pace quickened.

In the fall of the year, when the leaves were crimson and gold, and flocks of birds pointed the way, Harriet entered Maryland again to look for John Tubman. Time had softened the memory of their quarrels, and she hoped to persuade him to flee with her.

"John Tubman?" A woman in Bucktown shook her head. "He's married to a girl named Caroline — Jackson's Caroline. Lives up in Easton on the Jackson plantation now."

Harriet turned away to hide the disappointment in her face. That night she visited cabins in the nearby slave quarters, whispering a word here, a word there, humming a forbidden song. Before the moon had set there were ten men and women with her in the woods, following the North Star. The squirrels chattered in the trees overhead, and acorns, sounding like rain, pattered to the forest floor. A week later, they had reached Philadelphia and freedom.

In winter Harriet trudged southward through the snow, breaking off shiny icicles from the branches to quench her thirst, huddling in hollow trees for warmth. In the woods near her old home she found William Henry. Ax in hand, he was chopping down fir trees for the Big House Christmas party. Before he caught a glimpse of her, she hid in the bushes and sang:

> When that old chariot comes
> I'm going to leave you.
> I'm bound for the promised land.
> Friends, I'm going to leave you.

William Henry stood still, his ax in mid-air. He thought he had heard a familiar voice, singing a familiar song. The voice grew louder, and the song became a question:

> When that old chariot comes,
> Who's going with me?

Now he knew. Throwing down his ax, he shouted an answer to the unseen singer:

> When that old chariot comes,
> *I'm going with you.*

The bushes parted, and he threw his arms around his sister's sturdy figure. "Hat! Lord, but it's good to see you."

There were laughter and tears as the two talked together. "Ma? Dad? The boys?" Harriet's questions were anxious ones.

Rit and Ben were alive and well. "Probably live the rest of their lives in the old cabin," said William Henry, "but the boys are all over the Eastern Shore. I'm the only one still working here. And I don't aim to be here long."

"I'm aching to see Ma and Dad," Harriet said. "But it'll go hard with them if I do. You heard about me?"

"Sure have." William Henry grinned. "News about your last trip to Bucktown got around. The patrollers questioned us, threatening to beat us if we didn't tell where you were. Lucky thing we didn't know."

Harriet made her plans aloud. "Best to get started right away then. Know anybody else wants to come?"

"Do I?" her brother roared. "If you hadn't shown here soon, we'd of gone hunting for you. First off, there's my girl, Catherine. Skinny little thing, but strong. Mistress won't let us marry 'cause she belongs

to the Holdens. Then there's . . ." William Henry
named nine more men and women, all old friends.

Checking over the names in her mind, Harriet
nodded. "Tomorrow night's Christmas Eve. We leave
then, soon's it's dark. With the holiday all week and
plenty of rum and wine, they won't fairly get looking
for us before we've crossed the line."

In the Big House, Mistress and her guests were la-
dling punch from the silver bowl in the parlor when
the runaways took their leave. "God Rest Ye Merry,
Gentlemen" and "Good King Wenceslas" drowned
out the sounds of footsteps in the snow. Once in the
woods, with their breath puffing out in front of them
in the frosty air, the fugitives sang too, their songs of
Moses and Daniel and the Promised Land.

Toward dawn all songs ceased. The icy wind tore
through their ragged clothing. Feet were numb and
fingers frozen. Little Catherine, brave in a man's suit,
struggled to keep up with William Henry. The others
straggled behind in single file. A shift in the wind
brought a torrent of rain, soaking them to the skin.

"No fires." Harriet turned down their pleas. "The
smoke'd give us away for sure. Soon's we reach the
highway, there's a station run by a colored man."

There was grumbling, but Harriet's word was law.
Onward they plodded, out of the woods, over a fence,
until the highway was in sight.

"Hurry!" Harriet waited impatiently for the last

straggler before turning toward town. They must reach their hiding place before the sun rose.

At the first crossing, she stopped in front of a weather-beaten frame house. While her companions shivered in the middle of the street, she rapped on the door, once, twice, three times — the signal of the Underground Railroad.

But there was no answer. She rapped again and then again. Finally an upstairs window banged open and a gruff voice demanded, "Who are you? What do you want?"

Ten pairs of eyes stared up. In the gray dawn they could see that the face at the window was white! With a pounding heart, Harriet asked for the friend she had expected to find.

"Him?" the man at the window snarled. "Got chased out of town last month for harboring runaways." The window slammed shut.

With a jerk of her head, Harriet motioned to her tremulous party to follow. The man had been too sleepy to grasp the meaning of her question. As soon as he roused himself, he would give the alarm. There was not a minute to spare.

When they entered the town, Harriet had noticed a swamp with a small island of land in its center. It was there that she headed now. The pounding rain had melted the snow, and the group floundered to-

ward the island, up to their knees in mire. With chattering teeth and fast-beating hearts, they hid behind clumps of waving cattails.

The rain stopped, and the winter sun dried out their garments. Stretched out on the ground, they shared the food they had brought and whispered faint words of encouragement.

"Merry Christmas," William Henry grinned as he put his arms around Catherine's thin shoulders.

The long day passed. When the sun dropped behind the distant hills, Harriet crawled toward the road to see if the way was clear. Suddenly she ducked her head. A man was walking along the edge of the swamp. Dressed in black and wearing the Quakers' broad-brimmed hat, he seemed to be talking to himself.

"My wagon stands in the barnyard of the next farm across the way. The horse is in the stable; the harness hangs on a nail. My wagon stands in the barnyard of the next farm across the way. The horse is in the stable; the harness hangs on a nail. My wagon stands in the barnyard . . ." He had passed out of earshot.

Harriet crawled back to her companions to tell them what she had heard. "I'm going to go look for that wagon. Don't none of you move till I get back. If the coast is clear, I'll sing."

Minutes dragged by. Restlessly, the group in the swamp shifted position. The wind was rising again, and the cold reached into their bones. Then, above the rustling of the swamp grass, they heard brisk footsteps. Sweet and clear, a song floated toward them:

> Go down, Moses,
> Way down in Egypt's land.
> Let my people go.

The wagon was there, stocked with food and blankets, and Harriet had hitched up the horse. Before the North Star faded in the morning sky, the fugitives were eating breakfast in John Hunn's kitchen. With the wheels of the Underground Railroad turning, they were soon safe in a free land.

Harriet traveled to the South again in the spring, breathing deep of the smell of the freshly plowed earth, whistling with the warblers and the spring-peeping frogs. This time she was in search of Benjie and Henry and Robert, her brothers still in bondage. But they were scattered up and down the farms along the Bay. Before she could reach them, men and women stopped her, pleading:

"Hat, take me."

"I gotta go."

"Master's gonna sell me."

"Can't wait another day."

When she had assembled nine runaways, she turned to the North. "I'll be back," she gave a silent promise to her brothers.

The perfume of the magnolias was intoxicating, and Harriet conceived a daring plan for this trip. They would borrow a horse and carriage and ride in style. No one seeing a Negro driving a fancy equipage would suspect him of being on anything but his master's business.

Late on Saturday night a slave who worked as coachman hitched up his owner's finest mare to his owner's finest buggy. Clucking softly, urging the horse to a gentle trot, he drove to the edge of the woods. Saturday night and all day Sunday, Harriet and her party flew over the highway, defying pursuit. On the outskirts of Wilmington, they turned the horse into a meadow to graze, abandoning the carriage at the side of the road.

Entering the city was always a difficult undertaking. Even on Sunday the long bridge was closely guarded, and posters plastered along its entrance announced high rewards for Harriet's capture. After finding a resting place for her weary group in a nearby Quaker home, Harriet sent on a message to Thomas Garrett.

It was early Monday morning when two wagons

filled with bricklayers rumbled over the bridge. Heading from the city to the countryside beyond, the workmen sang and shouted as they crossed. Glad for the sight of friendly faces, the bridge guards waved to the cheerful crew. When they returned at nightfall, the patrolmen remembered them and passed them on without a search. Clattering down Wilmington's cobblestoned streets, the drivers pulled their horses to a stop near Thomas Garrett's house. Harriet Tubman and nine fugitive slaves crawled out, sneezing as they brushed the red brick dust from their clothes.

When he recorded the stories of these runaways in his journal, William Still added up some figures. "In two years, you have transformed forty slaves into free men and women, Harriet."

Harriet's eyes flashed as she repeated the words she had said on the day they met: "My people must go free."

Ship of Zion

It was a cold December day, and Bucktown's postmaster threw another pine knot into his stove before opening the letter he held in his hand. The letter was addressed to Jacob Jackson, an elderly freedman, and it was signed with the name of Jackson's adopted son, William, who lived in New York. After telling of life in the North, it ended, "Read this to the old folks, and give my love to them, and tell my brothers to be always watching unto prayer, and when the good old ship of Zion comes along, to be ready to step on board."

The postmaster scratched his head. There was something wrong here. William Jackson had no "old

folks" or brothers, and this nonsense about the "ship of Zion," what could it mean?

Sending for Jackson, he thrust the letter at him. "What's this all about? You up to funny business?"

"No sir. No, Master." Jackson read the letter slowly. Shaking his head in bewilderment, he handed it back to the white man. "Can't be meant for me, nohow. I can't make head or tail of it."

Once outside the post office, Jackson's footsteps quickened and he chuckled to himself. Harriet had dictated that letter. Harriet was coming. Her brothers must be on the watch, ready to join her at a moment's notice. Cutting across the fields, he hurried to the farm on which Benjamin was working.

On each of her expeditions Harriet used a simple disguise, sometimes dressing as a man, sometimes as an old woman. Now, as she headed for Bucktown, her bright eyes were hidden by the floppy brim of a sunbonnet, her broad shoulders hunched under a dusty shawl. Limping along, with her ticking bag swinging at her waist, she seemed an elderly granny on her way to the market place or off for a visit to her children.

As she neared the neighborhood of her old home, she stopped to purchase two live chickens. Carrying the birds suspended by their legs from a cord, she shuffled down the village street. She had almost

reached Jackson's house when, out of the corner of her eye, she saw John Stewart, whose fields she used to work. He was heading toward her. Despite her bonnet and shawl, he might recognize her.

Quickly Harriet loosened the cord which held the chickens. Off they flew, squawking loudly, while she gave chase. Doubled up with laughter, Stewart watched the little old woman who was stumbling after the lively birds. She climbed a fence, her shawl flapping out behind her. The chickens were still out of reach, but she was only a few feet now from Jackson's cottage. By the time Stewart had turned the corner, Harriet was shaking the old man's hand.

Jackson's report on her brothers — Benjamin, Robert, and Henry — was a dismal one. Within the last weeks they had all been sold to the cotton planters. Mistress was permitting them a final Christmas dinner with their parents, and on the following day they were to start the long chained march to Mississippi. It was now the day before Christmas.

"We'll start tonight then," Harriet decided. "Can you get word to the boys? Tell them, 'stead of going to the old folks' cabin, to meet me in the fodder house right by it."

Benjamin, always Harriet's favorite, was the first to arrive. "But, Hat," he protested, "we can't go 'thout telling Ma and Dad good-bye. They're old

now, and Ma'll cry her eyes out if we just up and disappear."

Harriet's eyes were misty as she put her arms around her brother's shoulders. "Ma cries, you say. But think of her wails if she sees four of us, and finds out we're all leaving. Mistress'd be down on her in no time."

"Last spring Daddy got a pig from Mr. Stewart," Benjie argued. "All summer long he and Ma been fattening it, giving it scraps they should rightfully been saving for themselves. Come fall, Dad killed it. For weeks now, Ma's been salting bacon and curing pork and stuffing sausage skins for a Christmas treat for us. Her heart'll break if we don't come."

"Lord knows I'd give anything to see them," Harriet mourned. "Anything but *your* life and liberty. Where you think Mistress'll go when she finds you're missing? Straight to the old folks' cabin. Without meaning to, Ma'll give our plans away. And get herself into a peck of trouble, too."

Sighing, Benjie agreed that Harriet was right. The two sprawled on the pile of corn ears, exchanging stories from their years apart. Robert arrived before long, bringing with him two men and a girl.

"John Chase, Peter Jackson, and Jane Kane," he introduced. "They got itchy feet. Jane here says her master is the worst in the county, but John and Peter like to talk her down."

"Takes a lot of traveling to find one worse than mine." John shook his head.

"I've heard tell there are good masters and mistresses, but I never happen to come across them." Harriet settled the argument with a smile. "Listen now, we start as soon as Henry gets here. What do you s'pose is holding him up?"

"It's the baby," Robert explained. "Coming right now. Soon's it's born, he'll be here."

"You're sure he'll come, leaving his wife with a brand-new baby?" Jane wondered.

"Just on account of that baby I'm sure." Robert nodded. "Henry says he won't bring it up to be a slave. Figures once he's free, he can come back. Wait for him, he said."

Harriet thought it over. "We'll wait. But if he doesn't make it soon, we can't chance starting tonight. Means we'll have to stay here till tomorrow night. We'll get mighty hungry."

"Plenty of food across the way." Benjie nodded toward his parents' cabin. "Suppose I go for some."

"Not you," Harriet decided. "Ma might wake. You, Peter and John, go in and talk to Dad."

The two men stole across the path and roused Ben. He returned to the fodder house with them a few minutes later. At the door, he stopped.

"Harriet, honey," he whispered into the dark. "Here's food for you all, and the blanket from my

bed. I can't come no further. Soon's she finds the boys
are missing, Mistress'll be after me. I'm not going to
see my children nohow. When the white folks ask, I'll
tell them so."

Ben stood outside the fodder house until daybreak,
talking to his children in a voice which cracked with
emotion, but never once looking in at Harriet. When
the first streaks of light appeared in the sky, he
slipped home, barely missing Henry.

"It's a boy," the young father announced as he
crawled into the corn. "Husky little fellow. Going to
raise him up to be a Yankee."

It rained all Christmas Day, and the seven fugitives took turns sleeping and keeping watch. Through
the chinks in the wooden walls, Harriet could see her
parents' cabin. Time and again Old Rit came outdoors. Shading her eyes with her hand, she took a
long look down the road. But none of her boys was
in sight. Disappointed, she retreated to her fireside
again. Harriet could amost hear her sigh.

Twice the fodder-house door opened a crack and
Ben's hand pushed platefuls of food inside. At nightfall he returned, with a handkerchief tied tightly
around his eyes.

"I'm going to walk with you a little of the way,"
he announced. "Give you a send-off. But I won't *see*
you."

Harriet threw herself into her father's arms. How

old he'd gotten! His once broad shoulders were thin and bowed, and his face lined with a thousand wrinkles. But the warm smile and the sympathetic voice were still there, and his step was firm as he walked along with them.

Benjie and Harriet linked their arms through the old man's. For an hour they led him, blindfolded, on the old familiar paths through the woods. Then it came time for him to turn back.

"Rit'll be looking for me," he explained. "Most broke her heart waiting for you boys today."

Farewells were brief. There was much ground to be covered before daybreak. As the party trudged on through the wet snow, Old Ben stood on the path until he could no longer hear their footsteps. Heading homeward, he comforted himself with Harriet's last words: "Be back soon."

When the slave traders, stuffed with goose and red wine, lined up their merchandise the following day, they found five men and one girl missing. The woods and fields were scoured, the cabins searched, but there was no trace of them.

"Not one of them come this Christmas." Old Rit shook her head when Mistress asked about the boys. "I was looking for them all day."

"Haven't *seen* one of them this Christmas," Ben agreed.

Because Ben and Rit were known to be an honest,

God-fearing couple, Mistress took them at their word.

The fugitives' trip was long and difficult. It was two days before the end of the old year when William Still received a letter from Thomas Garrett:

"We made arrangements last night and sent away Harriet Tubman, with five men and one woman, to be forwarded across the country to the city. Harriet and one of the men had worn their shoes off their feet, and I gave them two dollars to help fit them out, and directed a carriage to be hired at my expense to take them."

As he entered Garrett's letter in his journal, Still wrote, "Harriet Tubman had been their 'Moses.' She had faithfully gone down into Egypt and had delivered these six bondsmen by her own heroism. Harriet was a woman of no pretensions, yet in point of courage, shrewdness, and disinterested exertions to rescue her fellow men, she was without her equal."

The Old Folks

ON EACH OF HARRIET'S EXPEDITIONS, her parents were never far from her mind. They were both past eighty now, and although she longed to see them spend their last years in liberty, she feared that they could never survive the rigors of a trip on the Underground Railroad.

While she was in New York, still struggling to work out a plan for their rescue, she received an urgent message from Jacob Jackson. Old Ben was in trouble. A slave he had helped to escape had been caught, and had named Ben as one of his accomplices. The plantation owners were only too glad to clap Harriet Tubman's father into jail as an agent of the Underground Railroad.

Now there was no time for careful plans. Harriet needed money, and she needed it fast. With her ticking bag tied to her waist, she set out for the offices of the Anti-Slavery Society.

"Twenty dollars," Harriet pleaded. "That's all I need."

But New York's Anti-Slavery Society was not run by rich men. There was no money in the tin cashbox on the desk.

"No matter," Harriet insisted. "I'm not going to leave here, and I'm not going to eat or drink till I get money enough to take me down after the old people." And she seated herself in a chair by the door.

All morning and all afternoon Harriet sat by the office door, with the business of the Society going on around her. Fugitives were greeted and forwarded to the next station on the route. Newspaper articles were discussed and meetings planned. The room was crowded with busy men. Then the room emptied out and Harriet was alone.

Late in the afternoon, as she dozed in her chair, she gradually became aware of a stream of people entering the office. The news of her parents' plight had traveled across the city, and money for their rescue was pouring in. Coins clinked in the tin cashbox on the desk — pennies, nickels, quarters, dollars. By nightfall, when Harriet gratefully took her leave, she had sixty dollars in her ticking bag!

Once in Maryland, Harriet boldly made her way to her parents' home. Tiptoeing across the cabin floor at night, she knelt beside her mother's sleeping form.

"It's me. Harriet," she whispered.

Kisses mingled with tears, and tears with reproaches as Rit greeted the daughter whom she had not seen for eight years.

"Monday they try him in the courthouse," she moaned. "To spend the last years of his life in jail!"

"Ma, Ma." Harriet's voice was gentle. "I've come to remove his trial to a higher court. By Monday he'll be a free man."

Still shaking her head, Old Rit took Harriet to Jacob Jackson's house. Together the three made plans for Ben's escape.

"They don't move him to Cambridge till the trial," Jackson had learned. "Now he's in that one-room jail behind the post office. Take a man with a saw less than an hour to cut him out of that old shanty. I could do it at night, when the sheriff goes home."

Harriet nodded thoughtfully. "Ma, you got to warn Dad we're coming. Tomorrow, when you take him his breakfast."

"But the sheriff's there. I can't talk to him private." Old Rit was full of objections.

"You can sing, can't you?" Harriet asked. "Now listen." And she told her mother how to carry the message.

"Fine, Hat, fine," Jackson agreed. "But once you free him, what? He and your ma'll never make it North through the woods."

"You got a horse?" Harriet spoke quickly before her mother's tears could start again.

Jackson had a horse, bought after long years of hard work and careful saving. With a horse he could plow his little bit of land. With a horse he could bring his crops to market. In winter he could ride across the hills to visit his daughter and see his grandchildren. Without a horse —

Slowly he nodded his head. " 'Tain't much of an animal. But you can have him."

Harriet reached over to pat his hand. "You'll get it back. Or the money to buy another," she promised.

"Now," she turned to business again, "remember the junk heap at the end of town? Think you could get some of the youngsters to go there tomorrow and find me some wheels and two stout boards? We're going to build ourselves a carriage."

Buoyed up by her daughter's confidence, Old Rit sang when she brought Ben's breakfast to jail. Her voice trembled, but the words were clear:

> Good news, the chariot's coming,
> Good news, the chariot's coming,
> Good news, the chariot's coming,
> An' I don't want it to leave me behind.

Ben, expecting the usual storm of tears, stared at his wife. Suddenly he understood. Harriet had arrived to rescue him. His eyes lit up, and he formed a single word with his lips, "When?"

There was no time to answer before the sheriff shoved Rit from the room. As the key grated in the lock, the prisoner heard:

> Then lovely Fan, will you come out tonight?
> Will you come out tonight?
> Will you come out tonight?
> Then lovely Fan, will you come out tonight,
> An' dance by the light of the moon?

Ben chuckled. They made a fine pair, Old Rit and young Harriet. Between them a man could feel safe. He'd be ready tonight when they came.

At lunch that day the sheriff told his wife about his prisoner. "Those blacks" — his tone was contemptuous — "haven't any more feelings than an animal. Here he's due to spend the rest of his life in jail and he sits and laughs as if he'd come into a fortune."

At the other end of the village, Jackson's woodshed buzzed with activity. Wheels were rolling in for Harriet's approval. Wagon wheels, cart wheels, buggy wheels, some with broken spokes, some with missing hubs or bent rims. It was afternoon before she found two the same size in reasonably good repair. Origi-

nally part of a lady's chaise, they still bore traces
of gilt paint on their wooden sides.

Between the wheels Harriet fastened a rough pine
board as a seat for the passengers. Another board,
suspended from the axle by scraps of rope, would
serve as footrest. The carriage was now complete.

At the sight of the crude vehicle in which she was
to travel, Old Rit saw a thousand obstacles, a thousand reasons why their plans would fail. The tears
flowed down her cheeks in an endless stream, until
there were moments when Harriet lost patience. But
the long day finally drew to an end, and when the
North Star shone, Jackson set out for the jail with his
saw. Harriet, meanwhile, hitched up the horse. Together the two women waited.

There were anxious moments before footsteps
echoed along the path and Harriet again held her father in her arms.

"No time for talk now," she warned. "Before morning we have to travel across the state. In Burrsville,
on the Delaware border, a Quaker railroad agent
will sell us tickets for the steam cars. If we're there
by daybreak, you'll ride to Wilmington in comfort."

Before squeezing in beside her parents on the narrow seat, Harriet covered their legs with Old Rit's
patchwork quilt. This and Ben's broadax were the
only possessions they took with them from slavery.

Once under way, the rickety carriage flew along

the dirt roads, bouncing over stones, plowing through mud puddles, shaking the passengers until their teeth rattled in their heads. Jackson's ancient horse, accustomed to a leisurely pace, was lame and winded before they had gone halfway, but Harriet showed him no mercy. Slapping the reins against his haunches, she drove furiously onward.

It was still dark when the horse limped into the yard of the railroad agent in Burrsville. While Ben and Old Rit caught their breath and stretched their cramped legs, Harriet paid for their tickets and for the forged passes which would save them from questioning on the train. Not until she put the papers in Ben's hands and told him how to find Thomas Garrett's house did the old people realize that she was not accompanying them. Rit clung to her daughter, fearful of continuing without her.

"Course I can't go with you," Harriet scolded. "They got my picture at every railroad station from Richmond to the Pennsylvania border. You'd be caught sure, traveling with me."

In the distance a train whistle shrieked. Picking up his lantern, the agent prepared to signal it to a stop. There was just time for Ben to link his arm through Rit's and lead her to the platform.

"Now mind," Harriet cautioned. "No tears. You ride those cars as if you been riding trains all your life. Don't talk to no one, and when you get to Wil-

mington go straight to Thomas Garrett's. I'll meet you there tomorrow."

With a farewell kiss to them both, she was on her way. Turning from the highway, she followed a narrow rutted road into the woods. The exhausted horse balked and stumbled, but Harriet forced him on. Ahead there lay a grove of pine trees and a stream. The two drank greedily of the icy water before stretching out to rest on the fragrant forest floor.

As soon as darkness offered cover for her movements, Harriet mounted her board seat and headed for Wilmington. Ben and Old Rit were waiting for her when she pulled her vehicle to a stop outside Garrett's door an hour before dawn. Fearful that Ben's jailers might have already traced their route, Garrett had everything ready for their immediate departure.

"Thy horse is played out," he explained. "The livery stable down the street will buy him, and I'll send the proceeds on to Jacob. Thee'll travel now in my closed carriage. It's risky driving in daylight, but it's thy best chance."

With the two old people hidden in the back of the carriage, Harriet climbed into the driver's seat. Garrett had loaned her a man's suit, and she could easily pass for a coachman. While in Wilmington, she threaded her way sedately through the early-

morning traffic. But once outside the city limits, she urged the horse to a gallop. At any crossroad they could be stopped for questioning. Their safety lay in speed.

Tightly grasping the reins, Harriet drove on, faster and yet faster. The carriage roared along the road, leaving clouds of dust in its wake. Children with schoolbooks swinging at their sides ran to get out of its way. Farmers turned their produce-laden wagons from its path. Once a man on foot called to them to halt, but before he could stop them they were out of sight.

In an hour they had crossed the border into Pennsylvania. Still fearful of pursuers, Harriet never slackened speed. The carriage swayed from side to side, its wheels creaking now in protest at the crazy pace. Garrett's horse was panting, his mouth flecked with foam, when they came to a halt in front of the office of the Anti-Slavery Society in Philadelphia. Then Harriet's head tumbled to her chest and she slept, sitting in the driver's seat with the reins lying limply in her lap.

"The two travelers," William Still wrote in his journal, "had passed their threescore years and ten under the yoke. Nevertheless they seemed delighted at the idea of going to a free country to enjoy freedom, if only for a short time."

The Lion's Paw

T HE YEAR 1850, in which Harriet began her south-
ern travels, saw a great change in the operation of the
Underground Railroad. Heretofore, runaways had
been safe when they crossed the line which divided
free territory from slave. But in this year Congress
passed the Fugitive Slave Law, an ordinance com-
pelling sheriffs and marshals of the North to hunt
down runaway slaves and return them to their masters.
Under the new law, the fugitives were denied the right
of trial by jury; those assisting in their escape were
punished by fines and imprisonment.

When the Fugitive Slave Law was passed, more
than 50,000 escaped slaves lived in the North. They

had found jobs and built homes, and their children, given names like "Freeborn" and "Liberty," attended school and planned to become farmers and bricklayers and poets. Now their dreams were smashed. At any hour of the day or night they could be arrested and returned to slavery.

Thirty-six hours after President Fillmore signed the law, forty Negroes left Massachusetts for Canada. In the ensuing weeks the roads were jammed with refugees. Five hundred from Columbia, Pennsylvania; eighty-two members and the pastor of a New York State Methodist church; all but two of a Baptist congregation in Rochester. From New Jersey and New Hampshire, from New York and Pennsylvania and Massachusetts, black men were moving north. As they followed their star, they sang of the land where the British Queen promised freedom to all:

> I've served my master all my days
> Without a dime's reward,
> And now I'm forced to run away
> To flee the lash abroad.
>
> Farewell, old Master,
> Don't think hard of me.
> I'm on my way to Canada,
> Where all the slaves are free.

The hounds are baying on my tracks,
Old Master comes behind,
Resolved that he will bring me back
Before I cross the line.

I'm now embarked for yonder shore,
There a man's a man by law;
The iron horse will bear me o'er
To shake the lion's paw.

Farewell, old Master,
Don't think hard of me.
I'm on my way to Canada,
Where all the slaves are free.

Abolitionists, assisting "God's poor" and using pen and pulpit to fight slavery's evils, now found themselves in an undeclared war, with unfamiliar weapons in their hands. When United States marshals seized former slaves to return them, handcuffed, to the South, philosophers and preachers, writers and teachers battered down courthouse doors with axes and poles, and wrestled in hand-to-hand combat with police and militia.

In 1851 an escaped slave named Shadrach was rescued from a Boston jail and carried off to Canada; Jerry McHenry was saved in Syracuse, and Johnson in Chicago. More and more often a newly purchased pistol bulged in a man's pocket, and a rifle lay across his bed at night.

No longer was Philadelphia the terminus of the Underground Railroad. The routes stretched a thousand miles further north now, eastward along the New England coast and westward up the Hudson Valley to the Great Lakes and the roaring water of Niagara Falls.

Harriet was not safe when she passed the signpost on the border between Delaware and Pennsylvania, or stopped to rest in the shadow of Independence Hall. On her fourth trip from the South, when she brought out William Henry and Catherine, she led her party onward until they crossed the Canadian border on the bridge across the Falls.

"I couldn't trust Uncle Sam with my people no longer," she sadly explained. "They're not safe no more till they're under the paw of the British lion."

The trip across New York State in winter was long and cold, but there were friends along the way. Ladies assembled to sew warm clothes for the fugitives; men armed themselves and stood guard while they slept. A bookbinder in Troy built a hidden compartment for runaways in his wagon; an undertaker in Utica filled a hearse with live black men.

In Albany, Harriet always stopped with Stephen Myers, Negro publisher. In Peterboro, a hundred miles further to the north and west, her charges were hidden in the mansion of Gerrit Smith, millionaire

philanthropist. While they rested and warmed themselves beside his fire, Harriet told Smith of life in the South and her adventures there. The two became fast friends, and she never left his home without a handful of bank notes to assist her in her work.

In Syracuse, the Reverend J. W. Loguen, himself a fugitive slave, sheltered the runaways. Early in the morning in Rochester, they huddled on the stairs of Frederick Douglass' printing shop, awaiting the arrival of the Abolitionist orator and editor who had been born a slave in Maryland. Douglass fed them in his home, finding a place for them to rest on strips of carpet on the floors or in the hayloft in his barn. After dark he drove them to a nearby junction of the railroad, putting them on the steam cars for a through trip to the Falls. Their tickets were paid for with money saved from his lecture fees.

The last stretch of the journey was a tense and anxious one. Suppose the conductor should refuse to accept their tickets? Suppose the man staring at them from across the aisle should suddenly rise and denounce them? Suppose — But none of these things happened. The conductor was friendly when he collected the pieces of pasteboard which Frederick Douglass placed in their hands. When the man across the aisle rose from his seat as the train approached the suspension bridge, it was only to point out the beauties of the spectacle below.

Grasping William Henry's and Catherine's hands, Harriet looked from the window. Giant icicles glistened in the sunlight, and the thundering water, which even zero temperature could not still, roared over the cliff. Beyond the Falls was the new land. When the train slowed to a stop on the Canadian side of the river, a shout went up from the fugitives: "We're free! We've shook the lion's paw!"

Harriet's party joined a small community of freedmen in St. Catharines in the province of Ontario. They were frontiersmen, chopping wood in the ice-coated forest, frostbitten and hungry, defenseless in their thin garments against the biting wind.

Harriet was everywhere, that first winter, swinging an ax in the frozen woods, swinging a hammer on the cleared land. She cooked for her charges on a crude outdoor stove and washed their clothing in water melted down from blocks of snow. She nursed them, begged for them, prayed for them, fighting to keep them from despair by coaxing and pleading, by scolding and scorn.

"You say blacks can't stand this weather? When you were little, who wore the thinnest clothes, you or the white children? Who sat around the schoolhouse stove, and who worked outdoors in the rain and the snow? They had the cold in their hearts; in you, it's not more than skin-deep."

The long winter ended, and with the thaw the little settlement was a sea of mud. But neat wooden houses had sprung up in the clearing and a log road was laid so that wagons could enter. There were loans of seed from white neighbors; and when corn and wheat sprouted in the soil of Canada, the fugitives had taken root in their new land.

St. Catharines grew until its population numbered six thousand and it could boast a telegraph and railway junction. Harriet brought her other brothers there, and in the summer of 1857 she built a house for Ben and Old Rit in the settlement of freedmen. For William Henry and Benjamin, for Robert and Henry, St. Catharines became home. They were landowners and artisans now. They voted in county elections, sat on juries, and sent their children to school and church, alongside the children of white merchants and farmers.

But St. Catharines could not be a home for Harriet Tubman while there was still slavery in the South. She spent a few months of each year there. Then she set off again to shuttle up and down the land — from Canada to Philadelphia to Maryland and back to Canada, with a party of fugitive slaves. Eleven times in the years between 1851 and 1857 she crossed the border between the United States and Her Majesty's land.

The routes and stations across New York State became as familiar to Harriet as those of her native Maryland. Sometimes she made the last lap of her journey in a fishing boat on Lake Ontario or Lake Erie. More often she chose the train ride across Niagara Falls. As the cars clattered over the suspension bridge, she never failed to shepherd her charges to the windows to see the great waterfall and their new home beyond.

On one of her trips, Josiah Bailey, a giant of a man, sat huddled in his seat, still too fearful of capture to move when Harriet called. While the others stared at the roaring water, Josiah's shoulders were bowed, his head in his hands. Midway across the bridge, Harriet knew from a slight descent of the rails that the train had crossed the border.

"Joe!" she shouted, "Joe, you've shook the lion's paw!" Perhaps now he would rouse himself and look at the view.

But the words failed to move him. Again Harriet repeated her message, shaking his shoulder as she talked. "Joe, you're in Queen Victoria's dominions! You're a free man!"

"Free man!" Now Joe understood. He rose, towering over the others on the train. With his hands stretched out and tears streaming from his eyes, he began to sing.

> Glory to God and Jesus too,
> One more soul got safe.
> Oh, go and carry the news,
> One more soul got safe.

Every head in the car turned toward Bailey, and tears glistened on white cheeks as well as black. But Harriet still urged him to the window.

"Joe, come and look at the Falls!"

> Glory to God and Jesus too,
> One more soul got safe,

his voice rolled on in a joyous hymn.

"Joe! It's your last chance. Come and see the Falls!"

> Glory to God and Jesus too,
> One more soul got safe.

The train squealed to a stop on the Canadian side. Joe's were the first feet to swing down the steps onto free soil. The passengers crowded around him, and a young lady loaned him a handkerchief to wipe his streaming face.

"Thank the Lord," Joe beamed. "There's only one more journey for me now, and that's to heaven."

Harriet, at the edge of the crowd, slowly shook her head. "You old fool, you," she called. "You might have looked at the Falls first and gone to heaven afterwards."

Moses

HARRIET CROSSED THE LINE dividing the free states from the slave six times, twelve times, eighteen times, and the count of the men and women and children she led to the North ran into the hundreds. From Canada to the Gulf of Mexico, Americans knew of her plodding feet. They talked of her in the swamps of Virginia and the blue hills of Kentucky, and in Maryland's rolling fields. To the slaves, she became known as "Moses," and the stories about her became legends.

"Moses is tall — tallest woman you ever did see," a man said.

"Her eyes can pierce the distance like an eagle. Like a cat, she can see on the darkest night," a woman boasted.

"Moses runs faster than the rabbits, climbs trees like the possums, jumps over fences, flies over streams," the children whispered, their eyes big with wonder.

"She can hear a patroller sneeze twenty miles away."

"The fiercest dog will lick her hand."

These are the things the slaves said about Harriet Tubman. When she headed South, three words went ahead of her, buzzing over the grapevine telegraph until they became a chant:

"Moses is coming!"

Then, under the cover of night, dark forms stole to the woods to meet their deliverer. In the marshes along the Bay a slender ladies' maid named Tilly hid in the tall grass for days, on the watch for Moses. A husky field hand with a torn, bleeding back whispered in his neighbor's ear, "Next time Moses comes, let me know."

The slaveowners talked of Harriet Tubman too. "That black wench has stolen thousands of dollars of my property," one said. "We've got to stop her."

"Every time she steals five slaves, ten more take to their heels on their own. We've got to stop her," the others agreed.

"It now came to pass," a newspaperman wrote, "that rewards were offered for the apprehension

of the Negro woman who was denuding the fields of their laborers and cabins of their human livestock."

The cities of Maryland, Delaware, and Virginia were plastered with handbills describing Harriet:

A PLAIN WOMAN, SHORT OF STATURE, UPPER FRONT TEETH MISSING, WITH A HABIT OF ABRUPTLY FALLING ASLEEP. LOOKS HARMLESS, BUT SHE CARRIES A PISTOL.

Offers of rewards mounted from $1,000 to $5,000 to $10,000, until the "plain" woman who had been a "stupid" child and a "half-witted" girl was worth $40,000 to the man bringing her in, dead or alive.

These things made Harriet's friends proud and anxious. "What has become of Harriet Tubman?" Thomas Garrett asked William Still. "The last I heard of her she was in the state of New York, on her way to Canada with some friends last fall. Has thee seen or heard anything of her lately? It would be a sorrowful fact if such a hero as she should be lost from the Underground Railroad."

"She will probably be burned alive whenever she is caught, which she probably will be, first or last," the Reverend Thomas Wentworth Higginson wrote to his mother.

But Harriet was not caught to be shot or hanged or burned alive. Fearless, she was never reckless. Each expedition into enemy territory was thoughtfully planned and carefully executed, with a combination

of courage and cunning which would have done
honor to a general.

As a scout, she knew the hidden paths through
forests and swamps, and the houses which offered
shelter along the highway. She knew the potato holes
in the cabins, the secret rooms in barns, the hollowed-
out haystacks in the fields.

As a spy, she used disguises and passwords,
forged documents and secret signals. But these weapons of warfare were always selected with the greatest simplicity. A plain woman, she dressed plainly,
her disguise depending on a man's hat, an old lady's
shawl, a hoe, a broom, a market basket. Passwords
were drawn from the common speech of her people,
or from the noises of the night birds in the woods.
Her signals were carried by snatches of song, "Go
Down, Moses" and "When That Old Chariot Comes,"
with a change in words or a verse sung twice to carry
a warning to her listeners.

When she attacked, she made sure of taking the
enemy by surprise. On Saturday nights and in the
week between Christmas and New Year's Day there
were gay parties in the big houses. Masters and overseers ate and drank and danced, giving little thought
to their human property. It was on these nights that
Harriet held her parties too, assembling them by the
lights streaming from the curtained windows, march-

ing them North with the music of the fiddlers in their ears.

Harriet knew when to advance boldly and when to retreat. If slaveowners hired men to take up posters advertising her runaways, she paid others to tear them down. If the hounds were baying in the woods and the roads blocked by posses, she turned her party around. For a few stops she rode with them on a southbound train, confident that Negroes heading for the cotton fields would never be suspected of running away.

Strict military discipline was enforced while her infantry was on the march. Harriet was all kindness, yet as hard as granite. When slave mothers tired of carrying their babies on the long trek northward, she rocked them to sleep in the ticking bag tied to her waist, singing them lullabies as she strode along. Sometimes the infants, frightened in their strange cradle, cried in the night. Then Harriet dosed them with paregoric and kept them drugged until they had crossed the line to freedom.

She would carry exhausted men or women in her arms, bind their wounds, and deny herself to feed them. But if terror made strong men weak and brave women faint of heart, Harriet permitted no turning back. With her pistol at their shoulder blades, her voice was firm and her meaning clear.

"There's no going back on this road. Move or die! Dead men tell no tales."

There were no traitors on Harriet's trips.

Her greatest danger lay in her sleeping spells. Once friends found her dozing on a park bench in Washington, underneath a poster advertising a reward for her capture. On another trip she was riding a northbound train when she awoke to hear two men discussing her. To cover her confusion, she pretended to read a book which she took from her bag.

"This can't be the woman." The men nudged each other. "The one we want can't read or write."

"And I was only praying I had the book right side up," she chuckled when she later told the story.

Harriet's last foray was made in December, 1860, a month after Abraham Lincoln was elected President of the United States, four months before the guns of the Confederacy fired on Fort Sumter.

"She arrived last evening, bringing two men with her as far as New Castle." Garrett sent word ahead to William Still. "I shall be very uneasy about them till I hear they are safe. There is now much more risk on the road than there has been for several months past. Yet as it is Harriet who seems to have had a special angel to guard her on her journey of mercy, I have hope."

The fugitives arrived safely in Philadelphia and were sped on to Canada.

Harriet Tubman had crossed the line into enemy territory nineteen times, leading more than three hundred slaves to freedom.

"As a conductor of the Underground Railroad, I can say what most conductors can't," she grinned. "I never ran my train off the track and I never lost a passenger."

"The Most of Man"

THE STORY OF MOSES traveled across the continent to Ohio and Indiana and the plains of Kansas, where gray-bearded John Brown was fighting to make the territory a free state. It was told in the parish houses of Scotland and the English mill towns. Edinburgh's Anti-Slavery Society sent five pounds to Thomas Garrett to help Harriet in her work. Shillings were collected at a meeting of Manchester workingmen, and a Canadian school principal crossed the border with funds for another trip to the Eastern Shore.

But freeing the slaves one by one was slow work. "Like an attempt to bail out the ocean with a teaspoon," Frederick Douglass said. Men were coming

to believe that a faster method must be found. Up and down the land, a great debate raged.

"Slavery is a patriarchal institution," the South insisted. "Our Negroes are childlike and happy."

"Slavery is a peculiar institution," the North retorted. "It is against all laws of God and man."

"Slavery must be abolished!"

The cry was growing to a shout. But how, when, where? Honest men differed, and there were many answers.

"Outlaw it in the territories" . . . "Ban it in the South" . . . "Send the slaves back to Africa" . . . "Dissolve the Union" . . . "Preserve the Union" . . . "Vote the slaveholders out of power" . . . "Shoot them down" . . .

"Patience," men counseled.

"Action!" men roared.

As the debate grew heated, Harriet stood up to speak for her people. She came to the meetings now, unlettered, sleepy-looking, as black as her African grandmother. She talked at tea parties on Beacon Hill and at Fourth of July picnics in Framingham and Worcester.

"I grew up like a neglected weed — ignorant of liberty, having no experience of it," Harriet Tubman said. "I was not happy or contented; every time I saw a white man, I was afraid of being carried away. I

have seen hundreds of escaped slaves, but I never saw one who was willing to go back and be a slave. I think slavery is the next thing to hell."

"It's too late to send us back to Africa," Harriet Tubman warned. "There was once a man who sowed onions and garlic on his land so his cows would give more milk. When he found the butter was too strong and would not sell, he concluded to sow clover instead. But by then the wind had blown the onion and garlic all over his field. Just so, the white people brought us here to do their drudgery, and now they're trying to root us out and ship us to Africa. But they can't do it. We're rooted here and they can't pull us up."

In the South, Harriet's words added fuel to the growing movement for secession. Assailing as "traitors" those who "would laugh and shout over such wickedness in a poor, weak-minded Negro woman," a writer asked, "What could be more insulting, after having lost over $50,000 worth of property by that deluded Negress, than for a large congregation of whites and well-educated people of Boston to endorse such an imposition on the Constitutional rights of the slave states? Have we any right to expect anything but a rebellion against a government that refuses to protect them* against such outrages?"

* Meaning the slave states.

In the North, Harriet's words were greeted "with enthusiastic cheers." "She spoke briefly," the *Liberator* reported, "telling the story of her sufferings as a slave, her escape, and her achievements on the Underground Railroad, in a style of quaint simplicity, which excited the most profound interest in her hearers."

Thus Harriet became a symbol of her people in this great debate. To the slaveowners, she was "weakminded" and "deluded"; to the Abolitionists she was "the greatest heroine of the age."

In Maryland, men hunted her with guns and dogs, prepared to shoot to kill. In Massachusetts, she was an honored guest in the home of Ralph Waldo Emerson, the gentle philosopher; a friend to Bronson Alcott and his lively daughter, Louisa May.

When Old Rit complained of the bitter cold of the Canadian winter, Senator William Seward defied Congress and the law of the land to sell Harriet a house in his home town of Auburn, New York. Contributions poured in from all over New England to help establish Harriet's parents in their new home.

In these last years before the Civil War, Harriet continued to act as well as talk. Passing through Troy, New York, on her way to a New England Anti-Slavery Society Conference, she learned of the arrest of a fugitive slave. Charles Nalle, in the custody

of the United States marshal, was to be returned to Virginia before nightfall.

Harriet spread the news as she hurried to the courthouse. A small crowd had already collected outside the building, and she pushed her way through it. With her shoulders hunched and her bonnet over her eyes, she slipped past the guards to the second-floor office where the prisoner was being held. Crouching and shuffling, scarcely noticeable among the broad-shouldered men, she made her way toward him.

As she approached, Nalle wheeled on his jailer and ran to the window. Slamming it open, he stepped out on the ledge. From the street below there were shouts of "Jump!" . . . "Catch him!" . . . "Hurrah!" But Nalle hesitated, and before he could swing his legs over the side the guards were pulling him back into the room. While they snapped handcuffs over his wrists, Harriet cornered two small boys.

"Need more people," she whispered. "You go down and call 'Fire, fire!' The engine bells'll bring 'em out."

In a few minutes she could hear the clang of the fire bell. A swarm of men and boys following the engine down the street were stopped by the crowd in front of the courthouse. From the curbstone, a friend of Nalle's repeated in meaningful tones:

"Fugitive slave in there. Pretty soon you'll see him.

He's to be taken down South, and you will have a chance to see him. He is to be taken to the depot, to go to Virginia in the first train. Keep watch of those stairs, and you'll have a sight."

The crowd grew until a thousand people filled the street, blocking all traffic. Their angry shouts carried to the quiet courtroom above.

"We'll buy his freedom." A voice rose above the others. "What is his master's price?"

Nalle's owner leaped to the window. "Twelve hundred dollars," the Virginian called.

Worn purses clicked open. Hands reached deep into pockets. Pledges waved in the air. Two hundred, three hundred, five hundred, until —

"We have raised twelve hundred dollars!"

The Virginian's smile was scornful. "Make it fifteen hundred, and you can have him."

"No!" from a thousand throats.

"Two hundred dollars for his rescue, but not one cent to his master," a voice from the courtroom called. Below the people roared agreement.

Now the marshal made ready to move his prisoner. With policemen flanking him, Nalle was marched down the stairs. At that moment Harriet sprang into action. Straightening up, she ran to the window.

"Here he comes — take him!" she shouted.

Darting after the guards, she seized one policeman

and pulled him away, then another. By the time they were in the street, she had her arms tightly locked around Nalle's waist.

"Drag us out! Drag him to the river! Drown him, but don't let them have him!" she called.

Obeying her instructions, the crowd surged forward. The battle was on. In the first minutes of fighting, Nalle and Harriet were knocked to the pavement. Before they rose, she had torn off her bonnet and tied it on his head. Despite this disguise, they were shoved down again and again until Nalle's manacled wrists were cut and bleeding. Harriet's clothes were torn and even her shoes were pulled from her feet, but she never loosened her hold on the fugitive.

As bare fists flailed and policemen's clubs rose and fell, the struggle slowly moved toward the waterfront. The crowd was winning. At the corner of Dock Street a sympathetic boatman waited to cross the Hudson River. With Nalle sprawled out on the bottom of his skiff, he set sail for the opposite shore.

The breathless crowd watched the boat make its way across the blue water. "He's not safe yet," Harriet warned. "The marshal will telegraph."

As she spoke, the steam ferry at the end of the wharf blew its whistle. Time for the midday trip to the western shore. As one man, the crowd turned and ran for the ferry. Four hundred passengers was the

boat's capacity, and four hundred men and women steamed across the Hudson in Nalle's wake.

On the opposite shore, friendly hands pulled the fugitive from the skiff and led him up the steep riverbank. Before he reached the top of the hill, however, his way was blocked by a constable with pistol drawn. Nalle was again in the hands of the law. When the steam ferry docked, he was barricaded in the office of the justice of the peace.

Nalle's rescuers stormed the office, answering police gunfire with fists and stones. A giant of a man splintered the justice's oak door, only to be felled by a deputy's hatchet before he could enter the room. Stepping over his body, Harriet and another woman carried Nalle out. A passing buggy sped him northward, and in two days' time he was safe in Canada.

Even before the outbreak of the Civil War, Nalle returned to Troy. He made his home there, and fifty years later his fellow townspeople placed a bronze tablet on the site of the old courthouse to commemorate his rescue.

Harriet traveled on.

It was while she was in Canada, at the end of one of her rescue trips, that old John Brown sought her out. In the great debate, he was one of those who no longer believed in peaceful abolition.

"Slavery is a state of war," Brown insisted. "The slaveholders will never be induced to give up their slaves until they feel a big stick about their heads. We must oppose them with an armed force in the very heart of the South."

Harriet inched her chair forward as John Brown talked. On a map he pointed to the mountain range which stretched from New York through the slaveholding states.

"These mountains are the basis of my plan. God established the Alleghenies from the foundation of the world that they might one day be a refuge for fugitive slaves. They are full of natural forts, where one man for defense will be equal to a hundred for attack. They are full also of good hiding places, where large numbers of brave men could be concealed and baffle and elude pursuit for a long time."

"I know the Alleghenies." Harriet nodded. "But — "

Brown silenced her with a wave of his hand. "My plan then is to take at first about twenty-five picked men to the mountains. We'll set up our stations five miles apart. From these posts we'll go down to the plantations and persuade the slaves to join us. The most reckless and daring will stay with our band; the others will be sent north to Canada. Soon we will have a hundred men and twice a hundred, until our

fortresses reach from Virginia to the Gulf of Mexico."

Harriet's eyes flashed as she listened. The slaves would free themselves. This was her dream too.

"I'm with you, John Brown. What do you want me to do?"

For ten days John Brown stayed in St. Catharines with Harriet Tubman. Poring over his map, Harriet described the countryside where he proposed to begin operations. She located Underground Railroad stations for him, tracing the routes northward through Maryland and Pennsylvania. When he left, it was with her promise that the freedmen in Canada would join him to fight for their fellows in slavery. So impressed was he with her courage and leadership that he frequently spoke of her in masculine terms.

"Harriet Tubman hooked on his whole team at once," John Brown reported in a letter to his son. "He is the most of a man, naturally, that I ever met with. There is the most abundant material, and of the right quality, in this quarter, beyond all doubt."

While Harriet remained in Canada to enlist recruits, John Brown traveled through New England and New York. With funds from the Abolitionists, he purchased arms and engaged the services of a military man to train his troops. The blow was to be struck that summer.

Then came treason and near disaster. The military

man betrayed Brown's plans, and the undertaking was indefinitely postponed. As the months went by, Harriet's followers grew restless. Gradually they abandoned hope in John Brown's enterprise and returned to their daily pursuits. There were many schemes for freeing their people, and this one, like the others, had failed before it got well under way.

But John Brown had not abandoned his plan; nor had he forgotten the woman who was to be his lieutenant. Many times that winter they met in Boston, straining over maps, sketching forts, listing supplies.

"General Tubman is a better officer than most I've seen," Brown declared. "She could command an army as successfully as she has led her parties of fugitives."

A year passed and Brown, calling himself "Isaac Smith," rented a farm near Harpers Ferry, Virginia. As soon as men and arms could be assembled, he was ready to move. In the messages which sped back and forth between him and his Abolitionist friends, there was frequent mention of his "General."

". . . Harriet Tubman suggests the Fourth of July as a good time to 'raise the mill' . . ."

". . . Brown needs now only recruits to serve with him, and for those he relies on Tubman and the fugitives she had brought North with her . . ."

". . . Brown is desirous of getting someone to go to Canada and collect recruits with H. Tubman . . ."

The corn was ankle-high when "Isaac Smith" moved to his farm near Harpers Ferry. With his tall sons, he drilled in the fields, waiting. The corn was knee-high and the old barn stacked with muskets. Men joined Brown — Kansas men — but there was no word from Harriet Tubman. They were picking the golden ears of corn when the old man's son traveled to the North to hunt for her.

She was not in Canada. She was not in Auburn. From Syracuse, John Brown, Jr., wrote: "Found L. gone to Boston, Massachusetts, and also said woman."

But "said woman" was not in Boston either.

The dried cornstalks were piled up in the fields when Harriet's friends found her in an isolated cottage in New Bedford. She had been traveling through New England, collecting men for Isaac Smith's band, when the old head injury flared up. For weeks she had lain in bed, unaware of the world around her. Slowly she fought her way back to consciousness until the day came when she could sit up and listen to a letter.

". . . Remember the song about Joshua and the battle of Jericho? The walls will come tumbling down at harvesttime. Isaac Smith would like to see you . . ."

Harvesttime! It was now late in September. With trembling fingers, Harriet dressed. Disregarding the doctor's warnings, she persuaded a farmer to hitch up

his wagon and drive her to Boston. From Boston, a letter sped to Harpers Ferry:

"An express package is on its way to you. Wait!"

But Isaac Smith could wait no longer. Nineteen men, five of them Negroes, were living on the farm near Harpers Ferry. Curious neighbors might at any time wonder about this household of able-bodied men with its sheaves of pikes and muskets in the ramshackle barn.

Harriet was in New York, heading South, when the words flashed over the telegraph wires: "United States Arsenal attacked at Harpers Ferry . . . Slave uprising . . . Kansas John Brown holds Federal Arsenal."

The news gave her strength. But the next day other news came: "President Buchanan calls out Marines and Cavalry . . . Colonel Robert E. Lee leading assault on arsenal . . . John Brown captured."

The succeeding weeks were dark ones for Harriet and her friends. John Brown was tried and sentenced to be hanged. His voice was firm as he spoke from the gallows: "I am quite certain that the crimes of this guilty land will never be purged away but with blood."

In the South, plantation guards were doubled and redoubled, and runaway slaves relentlessly hunted down. Slaveowning Congressmen demanded the suppression of every antislavery voice. In the North,

people thronged to solemn memorial meetings in their halls and churches.

Thoreau, the philosopher, strode through the quiet streets of Concord, ringing the town bell, as he proclaimed, "Old John Brown is dead — John Brown the immortal lives!"

Harriet's eyes were brimming over with tears. "It was not John Brown that died at Charleston," she said. "It was Christ — it was the savior of our people."

The great debate was drawing to a close. A year after John Brown's death, Abraham Lincoln was elected President of the United States. Before he could take the solemn oath of office, seven states seceded from the Union. When Confederate batteries fired on Fort Sumter, Harriet thought of John Brown's words: "Slavery is a state of war."

It was spring when she stood on a Boston street corner, watching a regiment of soldiers as they marched off to fight. To the tune of an old camp-meeting song, they were singing new words:

John Brown's body lies amould'ring in the grave,
John Brown's body lies amould'ring in the grave,
John Brown's body lies amould'ring in the grave,
His soul goes marching on!

Glory, glory! Hallelujah! Glory, glory! Hallelujah!
Glory, glory! Hallelujah! His soul is marching on.

He captured Harpers Ferry with his nineteen men so true,
And he frightened old Virginia till she trembled through
and through
They hung him for a traitor, themselves the traitor crew.
But his soul is marching on!

Glory, glory! Hallelujah! Glory, glory! Hallelujah!
Glory, glory! Hallelujah! His soul is marching on.

John Brown died that the slave might be free,
John Brown died that the slave might be free,
John Brown died that the slave might be free,
But his soul goes marching on!

Glory, glory! Hallelujah! Glory, glory! Hallelujah!
Glory, glory! Hallelujah! His soul is marching on.

Now for the Union, let's give three rousing cheers,
Now for the Union, let's give three rousing cheers,
Now for the Union, let's give three rousing cheers,
As we go marching on.

Hip, hip, hurrah! Hip, hip, hurrah!

She stood motionless until the last "Hurrah!" faded
into the distance. Then, with her shawl around her
shoulders, she hurried off. Somehow, someplace, she
was going to join the Union Army.

Department of the South

F ROM THE DECK OF THE U.S.S. *Atlantic*, Harriet peered out through the morning mist. South Carolina was flat, its shore broken by twisting rivers and narrow inlets, much like the outlines of her native Maryland. But here palmetto trees with straight trunks and stiff tropical foliage grew down to the water's edge, and behind them gray-green Spanish moss dripped from the branches of the shiny-leaved live oaks.

"Alligators in the swamps" — Harriet had heard about this country — "and the fever they call malaria."

It had been a blustery late spring when she left New York Harbor. Now, as the sun swept the swirling

mist out to sea, there was midsummer heat. A warm wind brushed the water, and blue-green waves slapped the sides of the Union gunboats before breaking on the Sea Islands' sandy shores.

The quiet of the morning was shattered abruptly by the roar of cannon. Fort Walker on Hilton Head Island was saluting the arrival of the *Atlantic*, its guns followed by a fusillade from Fort Beauregard on St. Helena Island. These were the military establishments guarding the entrance to Port Royal Sound, once a major harbor of the Confederacy. Six months earlier a federal flotilla had overwhelmed the port's defenders and the Rebel forces had retreated to the mainland. Now Port Royal was a coaling station for Union boats engaged in blockading the South Atlantic coast.

With the flood tide, the *Atlantic* steamed upriver to Beaufort, headquarters of the Union Army's Department of the South. On both sides of the narrow river Harriet could see the old plantation houses set in the midst of flat fields of rice and cotton. But the broad verandas were deserted and the straight planting rows zigzagged with weeds. Flocks of ducks dined on the rice kernels, and nowhere was there man or dog to chase them away.

"Where's everybody gone?" a young lieutenant standing next to Harriet wanted to know.

"I hear they just up and ran when our soldiers

come," Harriet answered. "Hiding out in the back-country someplace, waiting for the war to be over."

"But where are the slaves?"

Harriet chuckled. "I guess when they heard about the soldiers coming, they just dropped their hoes and left the fields. Masters said, 'Run and hide with us. Yankees'll get you.' They ran all right, but they ran the other way. Thousands of them pouring into Beaufort and Hilton Head, begging to join the Lincoln army."

The city of Beaufort came into view as the boat steamed around a bend in the river. It was a pretty town, Harriet thought. The pavements of crushed oyster shells were gleaming white, and scarlet poinsettias and yellow jessamine lined the crooked streets. The big houses, two stories high, had spacious piazzas and ornamented columns. Even the slave cabins wore coats of whitewash, and their rickety doors and shutters were painted blue.

On the crowded dock, the line of blue-clad soldiers standing at attention was almost hidden in a sea of brown faces. As the *Atlantic* cast its lines ashore, a cheer went up from these newly liberated men and women. Another of the Yankee boats had arrived, bringing provisions and mail, and maybe guns for a colored army.

Harriet was one of the first to disembark. Shouldering her way through the crowd, she asked to be di-

rected to General Hunter's headquarters. Major General David Hunter, a former Abolitionist, was in charge of the Department of the South. She carried a letter to him from Governor Andrew of Massachusetts.

"The General? Right this way, ma'am." Half a dozen eager children led Harriet down Beaufort's main street to the plantation house where Hunter was quartered. From his veranda she could look across the fields to the tents which sheltered the enlisted men.

General Hunter's office was in the parlor of the big house. His plain wooden desk and chairs contrasted strangely with the polished parquet floors and ornately gilded mirrors, all that was left of the original decorations of the room.

"I'm Harriet Tubman, sir. I bring a letter from Governor Andrew." Harriet spoke slowly, unsure of her reception.

"Harriet Tubman! I heard you were coming." The tall man with the drooping mustache rose to shake her hand. "We can use you here."

Quickly he read through Governor Andrew's note. "Well" — he smiled when he had finished — "you've joined the Union Army."

"It's taken me a year to do it, sir." Harriet's reply was thoughtful. "Mr. Lincoln, he doesn't seem to want to use my people."

The General frowned. "It's a difficult situation,

Harriet. You and I, we see this as a war to end slavery. As Commander in Chief, Mr. Lincoln is afraid of losing border states like Maryland and Kentucky if he comes right out for abolition, or recruits Negroes into the Army. Even the slaves who've been left behind by their masters or who have run away to our lines can't be called free men. Right now they're just contrabands of war."

"Contrabands!" Harriet snorted as she warmed to her subject. "Can't win this war by half measures. Mr. Lincoln, he is a great man and I'm a poor Negro, but I can tell Mr. Lincoln how to save his money and his young men. He can do it by setting the Negroes free."

The General looked as if he was about to interrupt, but Harriet hurried on: "Suppose there was an awfully big snake down there on the floor. He bites you. You send for the doctor to cut the bite, but the snake, he rolls up there, and while the doctor is doing it he bites you again. The doctor cuts down that bite, but while he's doing it the snake springs up and bites you again, and so he keeps doing till you kill him. That's what Mr. Lincoln ought to know."

Hunter nodded thoughtfully. "Mr. Lincoln will see it that way as he gets our reports from the field. Why, one third of the population of the Confederate states are Negro slaves. Think of what a force they'd be on our side! Here I have less than eleven thousand

men, and I'm supposed to hold the whole seacoast of South Carolina, Georgia, and Florida, besides extending my territory inland. When I ask for reinforcements, you know what they tell me?"

The General had begun to pace up and down the room. "Washington says, 'Not a man from the North can be spared.' I answered them, by God." He stopped to bang his fist on his desk.

"I told them of the freedmen in Beaufort, and last month I formed the First South Carolina Infantry. There they are." He pointed to the window. "Drilling now, and eager to be led into action."

"But what'd they say in Washington?" Harriet was sitting on the edge of her chair.

The General laughed. "Congress told me I couldn't enlist fugitive slaves. Here's my answer." He picked up an official-looking paper from his desk and read aloud:

" 'No regiment of fugitive slaves has been or is being organized in this department. There is, however, a fine regiment of loyal persons whose late masters are fugitive rebels — men who everywhere fly before the appearance of the national flag, leaving their loyal and unhappy servants behind them, to shift as best they can for themselves. So far, indeed, are the loyal persons composing the regiment from seeking to evade the presence of their late owners, that they are now one and all endeavoring with commendable

zeal to acquire the drill and discipline requisite to place them in a position to go in full and effective pursuit of their fugacious and traitorous proprietors.' "

Harriet grinned appreciatively. "I've called slave-owners many things, but I never thought of 'fugacious.' Until they form a Maryland regiment, can I join the First South Carolinas?"

"I have other plans for you." Hunter shook his head. "You're going to be my liaison with the local people. They come pouring in here, new batches of them every day. Hiding out in the swamps, drifting down the rivers on rafts. Some of them are sick, and all of them are hungry. The best and strongest of them we want for the Army. Others can do laboring work for us.

"They don't fully trust me or any white man, Harriet. They've got to be fed and they've got to be taught. The plantations here must be put into cultivation again. There's work for a thousand Harriets." He threw out his hands. "But we'll make a start."

"Where do I start, sir?" Harriet's tone was businesslike.

"Spend a few days familiarizing yourself with the town, talking to the people. Then report to Henry Durrant, our medical officer, at the Contraband Hospital. You'll draw soldier's rations, but right now I can't promise you pay."

The children who had escorted Harriet to General Hunter's headquarters were still waiting for her. With them as guides, she toured Beaufort. Eagerly they pointed out the sights: the soldiers' tents; the parade ground where the new colored troops drilled; the big circular tent, looking like an Indian lodge, where the chaplain taught school whenever he was free.

"You learning to read?" Harriet asked.

"Sure we're learning," the tallest of the group proudly replied. "And our mamas and papas too. We're going to grow up to be free."

Everywhere there were crowds of ex-slaves. Some were watching the soldiers drill. Others were fishing from the old sea wall or the banks of the narrow river. On the outskirts of the town rough shelters had been hastily thrown together. The deserted houses of Beaufort were already filled to overflowing. Here the most recent refugees were setting up their homes.

At dusk, bonfires blazed in the contraband camp, and whole families gathered around to eat and sing and listen to the talk. In one group a woman was slowly spelling aloud. "Cat, bat, pat." She held her book at a slant so that the glow from the fire would brighten its pages.

Youngsters nearby were studying their reading from *McClellan's Bayonet Exercises*, a soldiers' hand-

book. "Advance, retreat, leap to the front, leap to the rear," they shouted.

A woman piecing together an American flag from scraps of old clothing held it up for Harriet to see.

An old man buttonholed her to tell of the Union bombardment. ". . . And now we's all free."

"We's all free." The words could be heard on every side.

"But 'tain't so — yet." A heavy-set man wearing the Union's blue uniform joined the group around the fire. "Not more than half free. Soon's I heard of the Yankees landing, I run off to join 'em. General Hunter gives us right good treatment. Promises us pay, just like the white soldiers. But that money never comes."

"I don't need money to fight the Rebels," a uniformed youngster interrupted. "Couldn't pay me *not* to fight 'em."

The older man nodded. "But you've got no children. Mine's hungry. They got to give our people land to farm and regular soldier's pay for soldiering. Until then we're not free. We're just — contraband!"

The woman sewing the flag paused to snap a piece of thread between her teeth. " 'The first shall be last and the last shall be first,' the Bible say. Our time is coming."

"Our Time Is Coming"

"Most of the people are very destitute, almost naked," Harriet dictated in her first letter to Boston friends. "I am trying to find places for those able to work and provide for them as best I can, while at the same time they learn to respect themselves by earning their own living."

Ranging up and down the coast, from South Carolina to Florida, Harriet organized classes in washing and sewing and cooking. She taught women who had been field hands all their lives how to keep house and how to make things which the northern soldiers would want to buy. With her own meager savings she built a community washhouse in Beaufort where the

freedwomen could earn money by doing the soldiers' laundry.

Her task was not an easy one. The contrabands were wary of Harriet at first. They had never met anyone quite like her before. Even her speech was closer to the Union soldiers' talk than it was to their own.

"They laughed when they heard me speak, and I couldn't understand them," she confided to General Hunter.

There were other barriers, too. While she drew soldier's rations, they must roam the countryside hunting for food. To win their friendship, Harriet soon gave up her meals at the Army mess. At the end of each long day she returned to her tiny cabin to bake pies and gingerbread and brew casks of foamy root beer. Contraband women sold these to the soldiers, earning enough to supply their own and Harriet's needs.

The work with the women was in addition to Harriet's duties at the hospital. Early each morning she made her way to an imposing white-columned residence on Beaufort's principal street. Inside, rows of straw pallets crowded the rooms, and the air was filled with the smell of sickness and the moans of the helpless and dying.

"We've everything here — and nothing," Surgeon

Durrant explained. "Gun wounds, malaria, dysentery, smallpox, and just plain starvation. There's a birth a day, and not enough muslin to wrap the babies in. There are dirt and flies aplenty, but no drugs or bandages."

"I'd go to the hospital every morning," Harriet later recalled. "I'd get a big chunk of ice and put it in a basin and fill it with water. Then I'd take a sponge and begin. First man I'd come to, I'd thrash away the flies, and they'd rise like bees around a hive. Then I'd begin to bathe their wounds, and by the time I'd bathed off three or four, the fire and heat would have melted the ice and made the water warm, and it would be as red as clear blood. Then I'd go and get more ice, and by the time I got to the next ones, the flies would be round the first ones black and thick as ever."

Harriet's steady hands and practical good humor brought her into demand as nurse among both contrabands and soldiers. When the summer heat became oppressive, a message came from Fernandina, a Union-held town on the coast of Florida.

"Our men are dying off like sheep from dysentery," a captain wrote. "Send Harriet."

In Fernandina, she found thousands of fever-ridden soldiers. From the roots of swamp plants she prepared a drink which cooled their parched throats. Sipping it, they felt refreshed, and they swore that it

was Harriet and her herb tea which were curing them.

When she returned to Beaufort, Harriet could see the change that the last months had brought. The contrabands were housed now in wooden barracks, with a room for each family. The plantation lands were broken up into small tracts, and former slaves tilled the soil which had belonged to their masters. But with a difference: the government established market houses for the sale of produce, and Negro farmers were paid for their cotton and rice.

Freedmen seined the island waters for shrimp and crabs, or ferried official passengers along the winding rivers. Others worked as laborers for the Army, repairing the docks and building breastworks when there was fear of a Rebel attack.

Harriet stopped to talk to a man who had been noted in the area as a "troublemaker." Now a farmer and a fisherman, he paid his debts and sent his children to the new school.

"When I first came here, they told me you were bad, John. How come you changed so quick?" she asked.

"Ah, mistress." John held his head proudly. "I'm free now. I have to do right."

Our time is coming. Harriet's heart skipped a beat as she watched the brown-skinned soldiers snap smartly to attention on the parade ground. The exist-

ence of the First South Carolinas was still not formally recognized by the Secretary of War. But only yesterday General Hunter had written to Washington:

"The experiment of arming the blacks has been a complete and even marvelous success. They are sober, docile, attentive, and enthusiastic, displaying great natural capacities in acquiring the duties of the soldier."

Our time is coming. Volunteer teachers sent by Freedmen's Aid Societies in Boston and Philadelphia arrived in Beaufort to set up schools where young and old alike could learn. They brought news to Harriet of changing sentiment in the North:

"Mr. Lincoln's saying we can't win the war without help from the slaves. Soon there'll be word of a new law he's writing. Slavery's days are numbered."

In September, when hurricane winds lashed the islands' shores, the word came from Washington. Abraham Lincoln would proclaim the end of slavery in all Rebel states on January 1, 1863. Slavery had only one hundred more days.

Our time is coming. The hundred days sped by. The traditional Christmas merrymaking was forgotten as everyone waited for the celebration which the New Year would bring.

On the morning of December 31, Union gunboats

steamed up and down the rivers, collecting passengers. Men and women traveled on horseback, in carriages, and on foot, carrying weary children on their shoulders.

In a grove of live oaks outside the city, freedmen built great bonfires, their flames blazing up to the sky and casting fantastic shadows on the gnarled trees. All night long beeves turned on huge spits. When the first rays of sunlight reached the blue river, the crowd began to assemble in the grove.

Women with gay handkerchiefs on their heads, and children with scrubbed faces and shining eyes, stood proudly beside their men in blue. There was a roll of drums, and all heads turned toward the platform. A Beaufort doctor who had long ago freed his own slaves stepped forward to read the proclamation of the President of the United States:

" 'That, on the first day of January, in the year of our Lord one thousand eight hundred and sixty-three, all persons held as slaves within any state or designated part of a state, the people whereof shall then be in rebellion against the United States, shall be then thenceforward, and forever free; and the Executive Government of the United States, including the military and naval authority thereof, will recognize and maintain the freedom of such persons, or any of them, in any efforts they may make for their actual freedom.' "

There was breathless silence in the grove. Throats were too choked for cheers. The commander of the First South Carolinas stepped forward to present a flag to his regiment — a flag made for the freedmen by a ladies' sewing circle in New York State. As he held out the Stars and Stripes, a voice broke the stillness. It was a voice which had been heard before, on lonely paths in the woods under the North Star:

> My country, 'tis of thee,
> Sweet land of liberty,
> Of thee I sing.

A quavering man's voice joined in, then two women's, until the whole assemblage was singing:

> Land where my fathers died!
> Land of the Pilgrims' pride!
> From every mountainside
> Let freedom ring!

Verse followed verse, while the officers on the platform stood at attention. Then Harriet spoke the final words of the ceremony: "This is the first flag we have ever seen which promised us anything. This is the first day we have ever had a country."

Mr. Lincoln's Army

AFTER THE EMANCIPATION PROCLAMATION, the War Department changed its policy on Negro troops. The First South Carolinas were now an official part of the Union Army, with Thomas Wentworth Higginson, former Abolitionist minister, as their colonel. Under the leadership of Colonel James Montgomery, who had fought in Kansas with John Brown, the Second South Carolina Volunteers was formed. A regiment of ex-slaves drilled in Louisiana; and in Boston, Governor Andrew called for the enlistment of two Negro regiments, the Fifty-fourth and Fifty-fifth Massachusetts.

Slowly the Department of the South began to push back from the jagged coastline where it was en-

trenched, to penetrate deeper and deeper into the interior of South Carolina. Although forces for a major advance were lacking, scouting parties traveled up the rivers to harass and capture Rebel batteries. Along with their guns, the troops brought word to the slaves of the President's proclamation.

"It is your duty to carry this good news to your brethren who are still in slavery," General Saxton announced. "Let all your voices, like merry bells, join loud and clear in the grand chorus of liberty. 'We are free!' 'We are free!' — until listening, you shall hear its echoes coming back from every cabin in the land — 'We are free!' 'We are free!' "

When the Army began to move inland, General Hunter sent for Harriet. "We need information, and you can get it for us," he explained. "The Rebels have no formal line of battle in this area. They're spread out in small groups, camping in the woods and in the barns and stables of the big plantations. We never know when a musket will fire at us from behind a tree, or a torpedo in the river blow up one of our boats. Before we send out our next expedition, I want you to scout the territory.

"We plan a foray up St. Marys River." He moved over to the map to point out the route. "Find out the exact location of the Rebel batteries, the number of guards at the bridges, whether the waters are mined.

But, Harriet" — his face grew grave — "you know the penalty for spying?"

"I've faced death before, sir." Harriet's voice was firm. "But never in a better cause."

Wearing a coat and dress of Union blue, and carrying a soldier's knapsack and rifle, Harriet set out. She had chosen to start at dusk, hoping to travel many miles in enemy territory before running the risk of being seen. The first hours, tramping along the riverbank, were peaceful ones. Only the peeping of the frogs broke the silence of the night. Then, a few feet ahead of her, a twig snapped. She froze, listening. Another twig. Now she could hear rhythmic footsteps. Through the leaves she could see a Rebel sentry pacing back and forth with his rifle on his shoulder.

Soundlessly, Harriet dropped to the ground. Slinking along Indian fashion, she reached cover in the woods without being observed. For a long time she crept through the underbrush before daring to circle back to the river. With the first streaks of light she turned inland again, heading for a row of tumbledown cabins which edged the rice fields. In the slave homes there was sure to be shelter — and information.

"Moses is here!" The old familiar cry traveled through the quarters. "Moses with a Yankee rifle."

Men and women gathered to hear her story. She

could tell them whether the grapevine telegraph reports of freedom were true. She would know whether the Yankees were going to sell them all to Cuba as their masters said.

"You're free!" Harriet had to repeat it again and again. "Mr. Lincoln gave freedom to everybody. And the Union Army's come to see you get your share."

When she explained the purpose of her mission, information poured forth.

"My brother helped build the Rebel fort at the bridge. I'll fetch him to tell you how many soldiers they got there."

"Every plantation along the river's got guards. Six of them quartered up in our barn."

"I can show you where they put torpedoes."

"Back in the woods there's a big camp — hundreds of men with guns."

By nightfall Harriet was ready to move further west. In her knapsack she carried a crude map of the district, marked to show the Rebel camps and outposts. After another night and day she headed back to Beaufort with the information General Hunter needed. Accompanying her were twenty-four fugitives, all of them eager to fight in Mr. Lincoln's army.

Following a successful expedition up St. Marys River, Harriet was authorized to form a corps of ex-slaves to assist her in her new work. The nine scouts

and river pilots under her command ventured far inland to report on enemy fortifications and troop movements, and to locate supply depots. When the decision for an attack was made, it was they who piloted the gunboats up the winding rivers, steering them safely past torpedoes and shoals.

"Next we should try the Combahee." Harriet was talking to Colonel Montgomery. "They have pickets posted every mile or two along the banks, but their camp is at Green Pond, far back in the woods. If we start at night, we could reach Combahee Ferry and the railroad bridge before the Rebs wipe the sleep from their eyes."

"How about torpedoes?" Montgomery asked.

"My men know where they are. We can pass them safely," she assured him.

It was a hot night in June when three Union gunboats left St. Helena Sound for the trip up the Combahee River. "First picket post 'bout half mile further, on our right," Harriet warned Colonel Montgomery.

"We'll leave a present for 'em," he grinned.

A dinghy put off from the gunboat to deposit five soldiers on the right bank of the river. In the moonlight Harriet watched them surround and disarm the Confederate sentries before an alarm could be given.

"Second picket post."

Again the men in blue were alert, and the enemy outpost was silenced without the firing of a gun. Two miles, four miles, six miles. They were halfway to their goal, with the Rebels still sleeping in their tents.

Now the invaders grew bold. Parties of men landed on either shore to carry the news of freedom to the slaves and to destroy Confederate property. Railroad tracks were torn up and roads blockaded. A barn piled high with cotton for gray uniforms went up in smoke . . . a warehouse stocked with provisions . . . plantation houses and barns. Long before the dawn, the sky was bright with flames.

The Union fleet proceeded slowly upstream, leaving fiery devastation in its wake. Steering past enemy torpedoes, they could see Combahee Ferry in the gray morning mist. After setting fire to the bridge, they turned and headed for home. The surprised Confederate forces were unable to reorganize their defenses. With a single cannon they fired at the Union boats, only to find themselves caught in a Yankee crossfire and obliged to retreat.

The trip back to Beaufort was a triumphant one. As news of the invasion reached the rice and cotton fields, slaves crowded to the riverbanks, following the sound of the steam whistles.

"Lincoln's gunboats come to set us free!" The words were shouted everywhere.

"Too old to come?" One white-bearded man shook off an overseer's restraining hand. "Never too old to leave the land of bondage."

"I never saw such a sight," Harriet said. "Here you'd see a woman with a pail on her head, rice a-smoking in it just as she'd taken it from the fire, young one hanging on behind, one hand round her forehead to hold on, the other hand digging into the rice pot, eating with all its might. A-hold of her dress there were two or three more, and down her back a bag with a pig in it.

"One woman brought two pigs, a white one and a black one. We took them all on board. Named the white pig Beauregard and the black pig Jeff Davis.

"Sometimes the women would come with twins hanging round their necks. I never saw so many twins in my life.

"The women had bags on their shoulders, baskets on their heads, and young ones tagging behind, all loaded. Pigs were squealing, chickens screaming, young ones squalling."

The dinghies ferrying the excited passengers to the gunboats had difficulty pushing off from the shore. Everyone wanted to get aboard at once; and as the small boats filled and made ready to depart, panicky hands held onto the gunwales. The oarsmen could not move.

Watching the scene from the gunboat's deck, Colonel Montgomery shouted above the clamor, "Moses, you'll have to give 'em a song."

Harriet lifted up her voice:

> Of all the whole creation in the East or in the
>   West,
> The glorious Yankee nation is the greatest and
>   the best.
> Come along! Come along! Don't be alarmed.
> Uncle Sam is rich enough to give you all a farm.

At the end of each verse, the enthusiastic freedmen threw up their hands and shouted, "Glory!" In that short moment the oarsmen were able to push off. Back to the shore a few minutes later, they took on another load of passengers, and another, until almost eight hundred slaves were safely aboard the "Lincoln boats."

Victory

FOR ANOTHER YEAR Harriet stayed in Beaufort, slipping behind Rebel lines to ferret out information, nursing the sick and the wounded, and shouldering a rifle alongside the men in blue. She was with Colonel Montgomery when he steamed up St. Johns River and captured the city of Jacksonville in Florida. She was with Colonel Shaw when the Fifty-fourth Massachusetts led the assault on Fort Wagner in Charleston Harbor.

The tide of battle slowly turned. There were Union victories at Gettysburg, Vicksburg, and Chattanooga. From Tennessee came word that General Sherman had crossed the border into Georgia. With an army of 100,000 men he was heading for the coast.

"Go home, Harriet," Colonel Montgomery advised. "Sure as shooting, Sherman will be in Beaufort before the year is out. There's nothing left for us to do here but hold the door open for his men."

After repeated urging, Harriet agreed to a furlough. She traveled North on a government transport, arriving in Auburn to find her mother and father ailing and full of reproaches. The ladies of the city had been taking care of them.

"But it's not like having your own," Old Rit was querulous. "You been gone too long."

"I'm sorry, Ma. But Mr. Lincoln sent word to say he couldn't win this war without me." Harriet tried to joke.

"Needed you, huh? Then where's the pay you get for fightin'?" Old Rit snorted. "That Tom Hawkins down the street, he been sending money to his folks regular each month."

Harriet's face clouded over. "You put your finger on something, Ma. You know, at first there was no pay for colored troops. Then, when they made us regulars, government offered seven dollars a month."

"How much the white soldiers get?" Daddy Ben interrupted.

"Thirteen dollars."

" 'Tain't fair." Old Rit shook her head.

"Until we get paid equal, we don't draw pay,"

Harriet continued. "Massachusetts Legislature offered their men in the Fifty-fourth and Fifty-fifth Regiments the difference between the colored and the white pay, but the men all voted to refuse. We wrote to Mr. Lincoln: 'We'll give our soldiering to the government, but we won't despise ourselves so much as to take the seven dollars!'"

"So now you haven't a penny to show?" Old Rit asked.

"Got a pocketful of papers." Harriet was cheerful. "Figure the government owes me close to eighteen hundred dollars, what with bounties and all. Colonel Montgomery's sure we'll collect some day."

Old Rit sighed heavily.

"Money ain't everything." Ben turned on her. "Harriet done right, and I'm proud. Did the Lord pay Moses for leading His children out of Egypt?"

Gratefully, Harriet patted the old man's hand. "But Ma's right," she said. "I been working without taking enough thought for my own family. I won't go back to war till I get some money together. We'll fill up the woodshed and the shelves in the kitchen before winter sets in."

But before the cupboards could be stocked, Harriet fell ill. She was close to forty-five now, and the years of exposure and ceaseless work were taking their toll of even such strength as hers. The sleeping

seizures became more frequent, until the day came when she could not rise from her bed.

"Hat's sick." Ben hobbled to a neighbor's house for help. The word spread through the city, and Auburn's leading citizens flocked to the little house on South Street with their arms full of offerings.

"Got enough calf's-foot jelly to take a bath in," Harriet grinned when she was well enough to sit up.

"And that's not all," Ben explained. "They been having meetings here and in Boston and New York, raising money for us. Mrs. Seward — she comes here 'most every day — says to tell you Congress just passed a law giving black soldiers same money as white. Paying 'em for all those months they fought without wages, too. Soon's you're better, you're to go to Washington. The Secretary's going to take up your claim with the War Department."

"Where's Sherman?" Harriet's first thought was for the progress of the war.

"Took Atlanta, and now he's marching hell-bent for the coast. His men got a new song." Ben's old voice quavered as he sang:

> Hurrah! Hurrah! we bring the jubilee!
> Hurrah! Hurrah! the flag that makes you free!
> So we sing the chorus from Atlanta to the sea,
> While we are marching through Georgia.

"I'd sure like to be in Beaufort." Harriet grew

dreamy as she pictured the reception that the First South Carolinas would give to Sherman and his freedom army.

It was February of 1865 before she was well enough to travel to Washington for reassignment. Sitting in Secretary Seward's office while he tried to straighten out her tangle of papers, she heard the booming of cannon. The Secretary's assistant burst into the room shouting, "Charleston is ours!"

Charleston had fallen to General Sherman. Now the cry was, "On to Richmond!" Already General Grant was closing in on the capital city of the Confederacy.

"If I don't move fast, they'll win this war without me." Harriet's face was wreathed in smiles.

"This is your victory, Harriet. You fought for it long before the rest of us did," the Secretary said. "I wish I could send you right back to Auburn now, with a promise that your pay would follow. But that's not the way things work in government. We'll have to put you in the Army again before we can get the money due you."

When Seward sent Harriet and her papers to Secretary of War Stanton, he greeted her enthusiastically. "We've just the spot for you. Martin Delany has been given a major's commission and authorized to go to Charleston to raise a regiment of ex-slaves.

The first black-officered regiment in our country's history."

He consulted a schedule of transport sailings. "There's time for you to say good-bye to your parents before you take off for Charleston. Get your travel orders here, and then report at the Battery in New York."

While Harriet was returning from her farewell visit to Auburn, a delegation of women from the Sanitary Commission came to see her. Throughout the war, the government-run medical and hospital services were primitive. It was the Sanitary Commission, a volunteer group of private citizens, who struggled to keep the camps clean and the hospitals staffed.

"The worst places in the country right now," they told Harriet, "are the hospitals at Fortresses Monroe and Hampton. Overcrowded, filthy. Children playing beside the pallets where their ma or pa lies dying."

Harriet explained about her assignment to Charleston. She was due to arrive there in time for the ceremonial flag raising at Fort Sumter. After four years of bombardment and blockade, the Stars and Stripes would again fly over the federal fort.

"William Lloyd Garrison's going to make a speech, and I'm planning to shout a loud 'Hurrah!' and 'Amen!' "

The women persisted. "More people are dying in

the Contraband Hospitals of Virginia than on the bat-
tlefield. Epidemics got everyone scared so we can't
get nurses or orderlies to work."

Harriet hesitated. The end of the war was plainly
in sight, and her services as a fighter were no longer
needed. But Seward had warned that if she left the
government payroll now she might never collect her
back wages. Her hesitation lasted only a moment.

"I'll go to Virginia with you ladies," she assured
them.

At the Colored Hospital at Fortress Monroe, Harriet fought disease and dirt as she had fought the institution of slavery. It took only a few days to organize an army of freedmen and -women, and to equip
them with their weapons, the scrub brush and the
mop. Like a whirlwind, she swept through the ancient building, cleaning what was dirty, repairing
what was broken, bringing order out of shambles.

On the day that Lee surrendered to General Grant
at Appomattox, Harriet reorganized the hospital
kitchen. When the guns of Fort Wagner saluted the
Stars and Stripes as they rose over Fort Sumter, she
was in Washington demanding more bandages, more
medicines, more doctors and nurses.

It was that night, when she was walking along the
Mall, that a shot rang out in Ford's Theater. The President of the United States crumpled in his seat with a

bullet through his head. In the mourning city, Harriet battled her way through War Department offices until she had obtained badly needed supplies and a promise of more doctors.

"But you're in charge of the nurses, Harriet," the Surgeon General said. "I've instructed the Department of Virginia to appoint you Matron of the Hospital, with full powers to enlist a staff."

By midsummer, the affairs of the hospital were progressing smoothly, and Harriet was bone-tired. "I'm going home now," she told the nurses she had trained. "Just going to sit on my porch and let you young ones run things."

Mounting the high steps of the train in Washington's Union Station, she was full of hope for a life of peace. As the train pulled away from the capital of a once more united country, its turning wheels seemed to sing, "We's all free. We's all free." Harriet dozed in her seat.

"Come, hustle out of here!" The conductor was shaking her shoulder. "*You* can't sit here."

Fumbling through her bag, Harriet pulled out her War Department pass. "Hospital nurse." She waved it at him. "It says I can ride half fare like the soldiers."

"Don't care what any paper says," the conductor growled. "No blacks allowed in here. Get in the baggage car!"

Harriet refused to move. She had fought the war, risking her life for men like this one. It was the summer of her victory.

"Pitch the Negro out!"

Passengers moved from adjoining seats to assist the conductor. It took three able-bodied men to pull Harriet down the narrow aisle and hurl her into the baggage car. For a long time she lay in the dark. Her shoulder was badly wrenched and her side covered with bruises. But worse than the bodily hurt was the bitter pain in her heart.

"All those years of fighting, and never a scratch from a Rebel sword or gun. Had to wait till I was coming home to get my first war wound," she brooded.

The Years of Peace

THE OLD HOUSE ON SOUTH STREET had been cleaned and painted. Starched curtains hung at the windows and the neat parlor was gay with floral wallpaper. Lawn and hedge were newly barbered, and the vegetable patch plucked free of weeds. Harriet sang as she brushed whitewash on the chicken shed:

> There's cider in the cellar,
> An' the black folks, they'll have some.
> Must be now the Kingdom coming
> And the year of Jubilum.

From his porch rocker, Ben called, "It's time for sittin', Hat. Come over here and just listen to the grass grow."

"Guess I still got to learn to sit," Harriet chuckled. "Seems as if there's always something to do."

For Harriet there was always "something to do." Within a year of the surrender at Appomattox she was supporting two freedmen's schools in the South, buying clothes and books for the students with money earned in domestic work and through the sale of vegetables and chickens. Her Auburn household had a habit of growing, so that there were always three or four or five dependent and ailing guests.

"Just lazy, that's what they are," Old Rit sniffed. "Can't take care of themselves, so they want you to take care of them."

"Ma," Harriet would protest. "Old Alice is blind and Susan only a baby. Three years old and no ma or pa. You wouldn't have me turn them out, would you?"

Her mother grunted. "They all know your heart's too big for your head. You never did have good sense since you was a child."

The peace was three years old when Nelson Davis lifted the brass knocker on Harriet's front door. The two had met in Beaufort, where Davis was a private in the Eighth United States Colored Infantry Volunteers. He was broad-shouldered and handsome, fifteen years Harriet's junior. During the war, he had contracted tuberculosis. Now, like blind Alice and Baby Susan, he was looking for a home in which to stay.

Despite Old Rit's mutterings, Harriet laid a place
at her table for Nelson Davis. Rest and good food and
the bracing air of northern New York slowed down
the progress of his disease, until he was able to
spend part of each day at his mason's trade. Harriet
helped him to establish a brickyard, sometimes working at his side, making bricks.

The spring in the North was cold, and in March the
crocuses were just breakng through the ground.
Harriet thought back to another spring, twenty-five
years ago, when the lanes were pink with magnolias
and the mockingbirds sang. John Tubman, laughing
John Tubman, was dead — shot last year in an argument with a plantation owner. Nelson, who was kind
and good, needed her help.

March was blustery, and a lone robin cheeped
from a tree in the yard when an Auburn newspaper
reported:

"Before a large and very select audience, Harriet
Tubman took unto herself a husband and made one
Nelson Davis a happy man. Ladies and gentlemen
who were interested in Harriet, and who for years
had advised and assisted her, came to see her married."

The next years were bittersweet, glad and sad. Old
Rit and Ben died in the '70s, proudly calling themselves centenarians. Nelson lived until 1888. After his

death, William Henry, a widower now, came to stay with Harriet. There was a constant procession still of the orphaned and lame, the helpless and the hungry.

"Can't turn 'em away." Harriet shook her head. "They've no place else to go."

Even in these years, Harriet did not learn to sit. Active in the fight for women's rights, she spoke from the same platform as Elizabeth Cady Stanton and Susan B. Anthony, suffragette leaders. She helped to build the African Methodist Episcopal Zion Church and participated in the temperance movement. Although she gradually outlived most of her Abolitionist friends, she still made week-end trips to Boston and New York to raise money for her schools in the South and to visit the Alcotts or Colonel Higginson.

With her chief source of income coming from the farm produce she raised and peddled from door to door in Auburn, there was a constant struggle to make ends meet. Sometimes the cupboards in the little house on South Street were bare and Harriet had to visit neighbors, with her arm thrust through the handle of her market basket, to get vegetables for a soup or a few pennies to tide her over. The food and money were borrowed, never begged, and they were carefully repaid when crops were sold or a donation from Boston arrived.

When the mortgage payments on her home were

so long overdue that the bank threatened to evict her
and her brood, a sympathetic neighbor, Mrs. Sarah
Hopkins Bradford, wrote the story of Harriet's life.
With money from Wendell Phillips, Gerrit Smith,
and a host of prominent Auburnians, she published
Scenes in the Life of Harriet Tubman. The book sold
well, and Harriet received twelve hundred dollars —
more than enough to pay off her debt to the bank.

But between the schools in the South and the
needy who crowded into her warm kitchen, Harriet's
money quickly slipped through her fingers. As it became increasingly difficult for her to earn a living,
her friends pressed her claims against the government for back soldier's pay or a pension. With an imposing collection of documents from generals and
Cabinet members, Harriet petitioned Congress:

"My claim against the United States is for three
years' service as nurse and cook in hospitals, and as
commander of several men (eight or nine) as scouts
during the late War of Rebellion, under directions and
orders of Edwin M. Stanton, Secretary of War, and of
several generals. I claim for my services above named
the sum of eighteen hundred dollars."

The first government money came in 1890 in the
form of a pension of eight dollars a month.

Eight dollars didn't go far, and year after year
Congressmen from New York State took up Harriet's

cause. At last, in 1898, Congress passed a bill which increased her pension to twenty dollars monthly.

Even before receiving the increased pension, Harriet had added to her financial problems. Her house had long been too small for the needy who applied at her door. Beyond her yard there stretched twenty-five acres of rich farmland with two houses on it.

"A perfect place for an old folks' home. The John Brown Home," she dreamed. "The houses could be fixed up and a community farm on that bottom land would just about support itself."

When she learned that the farm was to be sold at public auction, she tied on her bonnet determinedly and marched up the street. Several hours later she returned, the owner of the twenty-five acres. The bank gave her a mortgage and she struggled to pay the interest on it until she deeded the Home to the American Methodist Episcopal Zion Church several years later.

By the end of the nineteenth century, Harriet was a legendary figure. The children of the Abolitionists made pilgrimages to Auburn, bringing along their children to shake hands with "Aunt Harriet."

The mail to the house on South Street was heavy, and neighborhood boys and girls argued over the stamps from far-off countries.

"Here's a fancy one for you." The postman

knocked on the door one summer morning. "All covered with red sealing wax with little crowns stamped in it."

"Where's it from?" Harriet wondered.

"England." The postman had no intention of leaving until Harriet opened the package. Using his knife, she cut through the official-looking seals. Inside, there were two boxes and a letter.

"You read it, Tom," Harriet suggested.

Hastily the postman looked over the document, hunting for a signature. "It's from" — he hesitated over the strange writing — "Victoria Regina."

Harriet shook her head. "Don't know anyone by that name."

"Whoah! I get it now." Tom was excited. "This Victoria Regina — she's Queen Victoria. Queen of England! She says she read Mrs. Bradford's book about you, and she wants to congratulate you on your work for the Negro people. She would like you to come visit her in London for her birthday."

"That's right nice, isn't it?" Harriet nodded. "She's the one we used to sing about:

> Oh, I heard Queen Victoria say,
> That if we would forsake
> Our native land of slavery,
> And come across the lake —

"But what's in the boxes?" Tom interrupted.

Together they opened them. Harriet unfolded a black silk shawl while Tom studied a medal which showed the Queen and her family.

"It's her Diamond Jubilee medal," he read from the inscription. "Celebrating her being on the throne for sixty years."

When the news of the Queen's package spread through the city, visitors thronged to South Street to pronounce the medal "real silver" and the shawl "real silk." "The letter was worn to a shadow, so many people read it," Harriet told Mrs. Bradford. As late as 1910, when she heard of the coronation of George V, she asked a friend to congratulate the new King in her name.

Harriet hobbled into the twentieth century, making her way along Auburn's tree-shaded streets with the royal shawl around her shoulders. Wrinkled and gray, her body seemed to have shriveled, so that for the first time friends were aware of her small stature. Years earlier a Boston surgeon had operated on her skull. "Raised it up so it feels more comfortable," she explained. But the sleeping spells persisted, and a crippling rheumatism was slowly depriving her of the use of her legs.

Even when she was confined to a wheel chair, Harriet refused to be treated as an invalid. She could still talk and sing, and with her bright eyes and rich

chuckle she managed to dominate every gathering.

"Tell us about the war, Aunt Harriet," her great-grandnieces and nephews begged. The Spanish-American War had come and gone, but "the war" in Harriet Tubman's household meant the war for freedom of the slaves.

Rocking back and forth in her wheel chair, Harriet sang "John Brown's Body" and "Go Down, Moses." She pounded out the rhythm on her knees or clapped her hands as she went through verse after verse.

"And then, children, I crawled along on my belly like a snake." Now she was describing how she hid from Rebel sentries. Before her audience realized her intent, she had slipped from her chair and was gliding over the grass in her garden, dragging her crippled legs behind her.

"That's the way the Indians used to do it. Learned that from my daddy when I was 'bout your age."

It was not until the winter of 1913 when she was, by her own estimate, ninety-three years old, that Harriet agreed to remain in bed. Even then she received visitors in her room and had the newspapers read to her daily. As she followed the news of the suffragettes who were close to winning the right to vote, she sent a message to the women to "stand together."

Early in March, her breathing became rough and

her bright eyes glazed with fever. "It's the pneumonia, isn't it, Doctor?" Her voice was faint but steady.

Wordlessly the doctor nodded.

"Tell William Henry. He knows what people to bring to say good-bye. And the minister."

With her friends around her, Harriet joined in a prayer. "Now a song," she whispered. Her thin hands waved feebly as she led the group in singing:

> Swing low, sweet chariot,
> Comin' for to carry me home.

It was dusk, and the North Star was shining in the darkening sky, when her eyes closed for the last time.